Totally Cool
GrandParenting

▼

ALSO BY LESLIE LINSLEY

Leslie Linsley's Quick Christmas Decorating Ideas
Leslie Linsley's 15-Minute Decorating Ideas
Leslie Linsley's Country Christmas Crafts
Leslie Linsley's Weekend Decorating
Nantucket Style
Key West Houses
Hooked Rugs
The Weekend Quilt
More Weekend Quilts
A Quilter's Country Christmas
Country Weekend Patchwork Quilts
First Steps in Quilting
First Steps in Stenciling
First Steps in Counted Cross-Stitch
America's Favorite Quilts
Country Decorating with Fabric Crafts
A Rainbow of Afghans
Carry-Along Crochet
Quick and Easy Knit & Crochet
Afghans to Knit & Crochet
Leslie Linsley's Christmas Ornaments and Stockings
Leslie Linsley's Night Before Christmas Craft Book
Custom Made
Making It Personal with Monograms, Initials, and Names
Army/Navy Surplus: A Decorating Source
The Great Bazaar
Million Dollar Projects from the 5 & 10¢ Store
Photocrafts
New Ideas for Old Furniture
Fabulous Furniture Decorations
Decoupage: A New Look at an Old Craft
The Decoupage Workshop
Decoupage on . . . Wood, Metal, Glass
Wildcrafts
Decoupage for Young Crafters
Air Crafts: Playthings to Make & Fly
Scrimshaw: A Traditional Folk Art, a Contemporary Craft

Totally Cool
GrandParenting

A Practical Handbook of Time-Tested Tips,
Activities, and Memorable Moments to Share—
for the Modern Grandparent

Leslie Linsley

Illustrations by Jon Aron

St. Martin's Griffin
New York

Illustrations copyright © 1997 by Jon Aron

Designed by Patrice Sheridan

Library of Congress Cataloging-in-Publication Data

Linsley, Leslie.
    Totally cool grandparenting : a practical handbook of time-tested tips, activities, and memorable moments to share—for the modern grandparent / Leslie Linsley.
        p.   cm.
    ISBN 0-312-17047-5
    1. Grandparenting—United States. 2. Grandparents—United States—Attitudes. 3. Grandparents—United States—Psychology. I. Title.
HQ759.9.L55   1997
306.874'5—dc21   97-18978
                                                                              CIP

First St. Martin's Griffin Edition: September 1997

10   9   8   7   6   5   4   3   2   1

▼

For my grandchildren,

Andrew, Sara, Victoria, Tyler, Julia, and Cody

Contents

Acknowledgments

Thanks to all the grandparents who joyfully shared their grandparenting experiences. They are among the really coolest grandparents I have ever met, except for my own Nana and Gramp, who were the best inspirations for grandparenting. Thanks also to the parents of my grandchildren: Lisa and David, Amy and Stefan, Robby and Doug; as well as to my mother and Jon's mother and aunts.

Introduction

There are no sweeter words in the English language than "Congratulations! You're going to be a grandparent." Becoming a parent for the first time creates feelings of excitement and terror. But becoming a grandparent is pure bliss. It's an opportunity to relive a wonderful experience from the vantage point of experience. Once again you'll know the joy of holding a newborn infant, this time a child of your child. More than ever before you truly understand the saying, "All good things come in small packages." Shopping for baby clothes brings a whole new meaning to the shopping experience.

Once you've become a grandparent you'll gladly cancel a tennis game or a hair appointment when asked to babysit. You'll refine the art of baby talk and find that staring at a sleeping infant for hours on end is a most pleasurable way to spend time. Everything your grandchild does suggests that he or she is brilliant.

Today's grandparents are doing a lot to dispel the stereotypical images of silver-haired folks who fall asleep on the sofa or sit crocheting in a rocking chair. While they still give old-fashioned love and often advice, they take a more youthful approach to grandparenting. Many grandparents say they dislike being called Grandma or Grandpa because it makes them sound older than they feel. Grandparents today are leading active lives, many still going to full-time jobs, yet they are making time for good-quality grandparenting and finding it enormously satisfying.

While working on this book, I talked to hundreds of grandparents. I called old friends, casual acquaintances, people I hadn't seen for years. I talked to people on planes, in stores, at nursery and elementary schools, on-line, and anywhere else I happened to be. What I discovered is that every grandparent loves talking about his or her grandchildren and sharing grandparenting experiences. In order to present the most common problems between multi-generational families, I also spoke to the parents of the grandchildren about how they viewed their parents as grandparents. Then I found grandparents who seemed to be dealing with these problems in mature, responsible, and loving ways. In this regard, the book became a real sharing of ideas for grandparenting in today's society.

Our own grandchildren, ranging in age from one to ten, were the source of a lot of material. When I started working on the book, Andrew, the oldest, often showed up at our house after school. One day I said, "Andrew, since you seem to be over here all the time, how would you like a job?" "Sure," he answered. "Good," I said. "What can you do?" He thought about this, then said, "I can cook, I can bake, I can do crafts. Come to think of it, I'd make a pretty good grandma."

When I was finishing the book, I noticed he wasn't coming around as much. I called to inquire about his whereabouts, and he told me he'd been going to his other grandma's house after school because she's into making doughnuts. Then he asked how the book was coming along. When I remarked that I'd talked to some pretty cool grandparents, he said, "If you want to know how to be a totally cool grandparent, you should really ask the grandchildren." I did—and you'll see their comments at the end of the book.

For now I have only this to offer as a conclusion. All grandparents, cool and otherwise, are complete pushovers and will do practically anything to hear those magic words, "I love you, Grandma. I love you, Grandpa."

Totally Cool
GrandParenting

▼

1

What Do They Call You?

Yes, you look younger than any of your friends. Yes, shopkeepers often mistake you for your grandchild's parent when you're out together. No, you don't have a single gray hair on your head. And, yes, your daily visits to Club Exercise are paying off. However, this is all wasted on your grandchild, who insists on yelling "Grandma" across the supermarket aisles for all to hear no matter how many times you've told him to call you LuLu.

What's in a Name?

When I was a young mother in the midst of raising a family, my best friend lived a few houses away. Our children's schedules were synchronized so we could walk and talk while giving our children a fresh-air outing in their carriages every afternoon. Now, more than thirty years later, we write to each other from one end of the East Coast to the other. Our letters are mostly about our children and our grandchildren. In one of my letters I asked what her grandchildren call her and her husband. "They used to call us Grandma and Grandpa, and I honestly hated it," she said. "Now that they're getting older, I suggested they call us Joan and Tom. They loved it, and so now that's what we go by. Even when they write, that's how they address us. I explained that since they're growing up, Grandma and Grandpa sounded a bit passé. I like to think they see us as friends."

Modern Grandparents

Mimi and Jon don't particularly like being called Grandma and Grandpa either. Mimi says, "I often pick up my grand-daughter from school or one of her lessons. I arrive in my Jeep, wearing shorts and with my hair in a ponytail, and, quite frankly, I feel more like her mother than her grand-mother. In fact, people are often surprised that I'm her grandmother."

Many grandparents who feel young don't like the ster-eotypical image the old-fashioned titles Grandma and Grandpa conjure up. Some grandparents have tried, in vain, to get their grandchildren to call them by their first names; others have done this successfully but aren't sure how it came about. Mimi says, "I'd love to be called Marmee, from *Little Women*, but this hasn't caught on."

But I Don't Feel Like a Grandma or Grandpa

Each one of my grandchildren calls me by a different name—Nana, Hannah (a variation on her sister's "Nana"),

Gran, Grandma, LaLa—and I answer each of them in exactly the same way, with utmost interest in whatever they have to say. The two-year-old calls both grandmothers Gamma and gets two responses at once, which is just fine with us.

A Nickname Is a Nickname Forever

When my cousin had his first baby, my aunt Helen was a typical first-time grandmother. The title Grandma made her feel old, so she tried to teach him to call her Helen. His version of her name was cute when he was little, but now that he's a grown man with three children, his grandma remains forever Hum Hum.

When deciding what the baby will call you, try to project twenty years hence. And keep in mind that you may not have control over the interpretation of your name. Tori calls me LaLa.

You Decide

My friend Ellie came into my store with her five-year-old granddaughter, Sarah. "Will you buy this for me, Ellie?" the girl asked, holding up a wicker doll set. "Do all four of your grandchildren call you Ellie?" I asked. "They know I'm their grandmother. I don't need a title," Ellie answered.

Most first-time grandparents-to-be wrestle with this issue before the baby is born. They don't always feel like grandparents, and this title suddenly makes them feel old. When our first grandchild was about to be born, we told our daughter we'd like the child to call us by our first names. She was hurt, taking this to mean we didn't want to be grandparents. Of course, what we didn't know then is that your grandchildren will often call you what they want or can pronounce, not what you tell them to call you.

Step-Grandparents

Nancy and Bill are boating people, and everyone refers to Bill as Cap'n. Bill is a stepfather to Nancy's children. Their grandchildren call them Nana and Cap'n. Many children today grow up with two sets of parents. When they marry, they are likely to have two more sets of parents. This leads to lots of potential grandparents, especially if there are great-grandparents still alive. In this case many families attach names to the grandparent title. For example, Jerry's twin step-granddaughters call him Grandpa Jerry. However, Jerry's daughter just got married, and when she has children he hopes they will simply call him Grandpa and call his ex-wife's husband Grandpa, followed by his name.

Long-Distance Grandparents

"We rarely see my son's children," says Harry, "because they live with their mother in another part of the country. We sign our cards Grandpa Harry and Grandma Bess, and their other grandparents do the same, with their names, of course."

Once a Grandma, Always a Grandma

My ten-year-old grandson, Andrew, often rides his bike down to my store in the summertime. The store is at the end of a gallery-lined wharf in the harbor, where leisure boats dock. The promenade is lined with crushed shells, so he is forced to walk his bike to the end. But, being a ten-year-old and impatient, he often announces his arrival long before he gets to the store and screams out for all to hear, "Hey, Grandma!" One day I suggested, "Andrew, now that you're older, why don't you call me Leslie? I think it would be more appropriate when you come down to the wharf." As he hopped on his bike he yelled back over his shoulder, "Sure, Grandma." Some habits are hard to break.

Later that day I was in the video store. From across the aisle I heard a familiar voice, "Hey, Leslie." I looked up to see Andrew checking out a video game. "How come you called me Leslie?" I asked. "Look around, Grandma. Everyone in here is a grandmother. Do you think I wanted everyone looking at me if I yelled, 'Hey, Grandma'?" Kids have their own sense of logic. We just have to hope it coincides with our desires.

Fantasy Meets Reality

When Susie's daughter had a baby at age seventeen, Susie was thirty-six and felt too young to be a grandmother. "It made me feel older in my own eyes," she says. "I knew one thing for sure—I would never be called Grandma. But when the baby was born, the reality of his existence was overwhelming. I found myself cooing at him and saying things like, 'Come to Grandma,' and I realized what an opportunity I had to enjoy all the most pleasurable things about being a parent again." Now she has three, and last summer she took them to Disney World to celebrate her fortieth birthday! And what do they call her? SuSu. "And would you believe," she says, "I keep trying to get them to call me Grandma."

2

Communication

There are all sorts of ways we communicate with our grand-children depending on their ages, how far away they live, and what technology is available. When my sister and I were growing up, my mother's parents lived half the year in Florida and half in Connecticut where we lived. From the time we were in elementary school until their deaths, we corresponded by mail when they were away, and when our children were old enough they too wrote back and forth to Nana and Gramp. My grandparents' ability to communicate with all of us—my sister and me, my children and hers—on the appropriate levels was incredible. I saved their letters and marvel at how perfectly right their corre-spondence was at any given time, both in content and length of communication. This is an art that came naturally to them, and I find myself remembering their letters as I struggle to connect appropriately with two-and four-year-old grandchildren living far away.

Now my mother lives in Florida, and while she doesn't write letters to her five grandchildren the way her parents wrote to us, and later them, she talks to at least one and often more of them by phone every week. As the next generation of grandparents, Jon and I E-mail messages to our grandchildren who are computer savvy. I hope this will affect them the way my grandparents' letters affected me. I can't imagine what form the future of grandparent-grandchild communication will take, but no matter what the method, it's a precious activity that your grandkids, and you, will always treasure.

 ## By Phone

Sometimes I answer the phone only to get silence on the other end. "Hello, hello," I say over and over into the phone until a little voice speaks up and says, "Hi, Nana." Sometimes we just hear heavy breathing. I have to remember in these incidents to ask, "Is that you, Cody?" until a little voice identifies itself.

Never Too Young to Sing Along

When Dan and Joanna had their first grandchild, they were overjoyed. They called every day to hear even the most trivial news. "Put the phone to her ear," Joanna instructed when the baby was only two months old. She sang a well-known nursery song to the baby. Both Dan and Joanna took turns singing to the baby every time they called. They did this right up until the child could talk to them, and now they sing songs over the phone together. Joanna says, "Now when I call her two-year-old brother, he says, 'Tell Grandpa to get on the other phone so we can all sing together.' " Singing together has become a tradition in the family. Dan and Joanna do this with all seven of their grandchildren.

Short and Sweet

Tyler, age four, knows the speed-dial buttons to press to call all his grandparents. When any of the four answers, he quickly gives his message, "Hi, this is Tyler. Bye," and hangs up. None of his grandparents tries to get him to say any more, because they don't want to turn calling into a chore. Just hearing his voice from time to time is fine.

Talk to Her Parents Later

Edwina calls each of her grandchildren once a week. When a parent answers, she makes it clear that she's calling to talk to the child. She has a complete conversation with the child, brief if the child is busy and uninterested, longer if the child is in the mood to talk. Then she says good-bye. She never asks to speak to the child's mother or father, so the children know these special calls are meant only for them. Edwina calls their parents at other times and loves hearing about her grandchildren's latest accomplishments. "Right now," she says, "my children are so involved with parenting that it's all-engrossing. I'm the perfect listener because they know I'm totally interested."

How Often Do You Call?

According to a recent AT&T nationwide survey of more than one-thousand grandparents, those between the ages of forty-five and fifty-four are twice as likely as older grandparents to talk with their grandchildren on the phone. Further, the study found that 59 percent of grandchildren frequently call their grandparents. Twenty-five percent never call, and 16 percent are too young to call. Not surprisingly, grandparents are more likely than grandchildren to initiate the call. More than half of grandparents surveyed call their grandchildren at least once a week, and four in ten grandparents receive a call from their grandchildren at least once a week.

Grandmothers and grandfathers are equally likely to talk with their grandchildren on the phone, and 21 percent call their grandchildren four or more times a week. Younger grandparents call more frequently. Younger grandparents also get more calls from grandchildren. The most memorable phone conversations between grandparents and grandchildren recognize holidays and special occasions.

What Did He Say?

Carl loves to have "conversations" with his two-and-a-half-year-old grandchild. The boy babbles incoherently, and Carl responds. If you ask Carl what the child is saying, he tells you he hasn't a clue. But this doesn't stop them from doing all sorts of things together while conversing nonstop.

Listen Carefully

On the other hand, Jon's ten-year-old grandson has lots to say and is extremely articulate. Listening to grandchildren can teach us a great deal about what's going on in their world. For example, the other day Andrew called to tell his grandfather about a book he was reading. It was filled with scientific facts he wanted to share. Grandpa was impressed with his ability to explain what he had learned and realized that Andrew's vocabulary and level of understanding had grown quite a bit. Our grandchildren are learning and growing all the time. By listening to what they have to say, we won't risk talking down to them and undermining the relationship.

Heard but Not Seen

Small children love to play peekaboo before they can talk. You can play this over the phone. My daughter Robby puts the phone up to her one-year-old's ear, and I say, "Where's Cody?" I pause because I know he's putting his hands over his eyes. Then I say, "There you are!" and I'm content to hear his little squeals of laughter.

Baby's First Words

First-time grandmother Mimi reports, "My son, Jim, called to say that our grandson had just said his first word. Jim put the phone up to the baby and prompted him to repeat the word. 'Say Dada,' Jim repeated over and over. The baby just chewed the phone and gurgled." However, Mimi assured Jim that she had indeed heard the baby say "Dada."

A Grandchild's Voice Is Always Welcome

There isn't a grandparent I know who minds being interrupted at the office to hear a breathing baby on the other end of the phone. Tell your children that a call from a grandchild is appreciated at any time. When the grandchildren are older, there are ways to encourage them to keep calling.

Stephanie is nineteen and calls her grandmother once a week from college just to chat. From when she was a little girl, she says, no matter when she called, her grandmother would say, "Stephanie, I'm so glad to hear from you. I'm so lucky to have you." Stephanie says her grandmother is always eager to listen to what's going on in her life and remembers to ask all the right questions to get an update on where they left off in their last conversation. Her grandmother is an executive in a very busy office and says she keeps notes on her desk about things she thinks Stephanie will be interested in and can mention when they talk. But mostly she knows that teenagers like to talk more than listen, and she's a good listener. "And there's one more thing," Stephanie's grandmother says. "A grandmother's job is to give unconditional love. Sometimes Stephanie asks me for advice. I try to give it as objectively as I can, even when I find the idea of a nose ring utterly appalling."

Special Events

Keeping abreast of your grandchildren's special events and things they are participating in will enable you to call shortly after the event to share in their excitement. I am always slightly jealous of the other grandparents who live nearer to my grandchildren because they can see them more often and plan special activities together. However, when Sara called to tell me about her trip to the circus with her father's parents, it made me part of the experience and I was able to share and delight in her telling of the event. It wasn't the same as having been there, but I was thrilled that she wanted to tell me about it. In the summer, when I see her more often, we do something special together and she calls to share our activities with her other grandparents.

By Mail

When we go away I try to buy postcards right away to send to all our grandchildren, but that's different from establishing the mail as the route to an ongoing relationship. Now and then I remember to send a silly card or drawing, but I must admit that most of the cards and drawings come from their house to ours rather than the other way around. Here's how some mail-savvy grandparents do it.

Scrapbooks

Helen sends her granddaughter scrapbook pages with photos, sketches, and clippings that show what Helen is doing, her surroundings, and activities. She also sent the child a pretty three-ring notebook so she could keep the pages as an ongoing chronological scrapbook. When her grandchild is older, Helen will encourage her to make her own scrapbook of her everyday activities and special memories to share with Grandma.

Building a Family History

It's important to keep family stories alive. One grandfather sends short tales about his grandchild's mother and father when they were little and stories about things he did with them. He includes photographs to illustrate the stories. These family memories are often read as bedtime stories.

A Good Tale Goes a Long Way

When my husband, Jon, was a little boy he rescued a baby squirrel that had fallen from a tree in his front yard. He nursed the squirrel and took care of it until it was grown. Gus Gus, as the squirrel was called, became his pet and got into all sorts of trouble. All the little grandchildren in our family love "Tales of Gus Gus" and can't seem to get enough. They never tire of hearing the same stories over and over. Each has his or her favorite.

The children have names for the various Gus Gus episodes, such as "Gus Gus Goes to School" or "Gus Gus Runs Away." Sometimes Pop Pop exaggerates a story and has been known, on occasion, to make up a new one when faced with expectant, eager faces.

If you had a childhood pet, collection, or hobby that you particularly loved, it's easy to turn it into an ongoing story to send to your grandchildren. I even know one grandparent who's built years' worth of correspondence around a neighborhood bully whom he's given a tongue twister of a name.

Keep It Simple

I've found that the simplest idea is the best. Small children in particular don't have patience to hear a long letter from Grandma read to them. Besides, most grandparents I know are, regrettably, too busy to correspond. However, cutting a bright red truck out of a magazine and pasting it onto a piece of paper isn't a big chore. Write across the top of the page, "I'm sending you this big red truck so we can take a trip together. Where should we go?" This can lead to all sorts of back-and-forth imaginary fun.

Pen Pals

Ruthie's grandchildren range in age from twenty-nine years down to six months. When her oldest granddaughter was in elementary school, she asked Ruthie to be her pen pal. They began writing back and forth regularly, and this continued right through college. "It's not easy being a pen pal," Ruthie says now, "but I cherish those letters and have saved them all these years." Last year this grandchild got married, and when she was engaged she wrote to her grandmother to talk about her wedding plans. Ruthie has a wonderful record of all her passages from childhood to adulthood in their letters. "Now," she says, "I'm writing to the little ones. They love getting a letter in the mail, each with his very own name on the envelope."

If Baking Is Your Thing

When my children were little they lamented over the fact that they didn't have a mother who wore an apron and presented them with home-baked cookies after school. They had a mother who, while she didn't go to an office away from home, was nonetheless not exactly available. Coming home to the sound of typing and reading a note not to disturb me, as I had a deadline to honor, was more the norm. So I am not exactly the cookie-baking grand-

mother either. In fact on one occasion when I was buried in my office, Andrew, then age eight, came in with a tray of freshly baked chocolate-chip cookies he'd made from cookie dough I keep in the refrigerator at his request. Being aware of the humor in the situation, he said, "There's something wrong with this picture, Grandma. The little boy isn't supposed to be making the cookies for his grandma. It's supposed to be the other way around." I didn't feel guilty when his mother said the very same thing at his age, and nothing has changed.

However, there are many grandmothers, my mother included, who have family recipes they love to keep alive. My mother sends all sorts of baked goods to her grandchildren, along with the recipes. They use these recipes often, the results of which they bring to me. A reversal of roles, perhaps, but who's keeping score? Some grandparents send goodies with a note enclosed, telling the history of the family recipe, and this makes them all the more special.

Share a Hobby

Tom sent a birdhouse as a gift to his grandchildren so they could experience what he enjoyed from his window. Later he sent them simple bird books to identify the ones their birdhouse attracted. His correspondence with them revolved around bird-watching, and when they were a little older he sent them binoculars. Now, as teenagers, they go on birding walks with Tom whenever they visit each other.

 ## By Fax and E-Mail

Children are computer savvy. They are quite comfortable communicating by E-mail, and once you get in the habit it's a wonderful way to keep in touch easily. Sara, age six, and her grandpa send each other messages through the computer. Her messages are short and sweet, "I love you Pop Pop," as she is just learning to read and write. It's a great tool for tracking a child's writing skills while she's learning to write more words and express herself. As she gets older, we hope she'll tell him all about her day at school and he can write back accordingly.

Making It Special

Today Jon opened his E-mail for messages and, to his surprise, received a picture. A whole new world of communication is opening up. If you don't have the know-how to download a picture (though you can find directions on-line or in a guide to the Web—or ask one of your grandchildren to teach you!), try using a "smiley" or two. These are typed symbols that help illustrate your message. For example:

    :-)   smiley
    ;-)   wink
    :-o   surprise!
    :-(sad
    {}   hug
    {{}}   great big hug
    @ }~~> rose

Punctuate your message with a smiley—or make up your own with your grandchild. (If you don't understand them, turn this book on its side.)

Fax It

When Julia goes to her father's office, she brings her crayons and a sketch pad. She draws a picture for each of her grandparents, showing what she's doing and where she is. Then her daddy faxes her pictures to her grandparents. They usually fax a message and sometimes a drawing back.

Together Separately

The other day ten-year-old Andrew came to my office after school. As usual, he went right to the most high-tech of our computers and turned on the latest and most challenging game. I was working at my computer a few feet away. After a while Andrew said, "Grandma, check your E-mail." I did, and on the screen he had written, "Grandma, aren't we the family of the '90s?" It was definitely a modern-day Norman Rockwell moment. If you don't have two computers, or your grandchild lives far away, try re-creating this moment by scheduling a time you'll both be on-line. You can chat with your grandchild in real time, typing messages back and forth. Do this in a prearranged chat room, or several on-line services provide a way to chat one-on-one. Call your server's help line for directions.

Times Change

Each of Maddy's sons has three daughters. The whole family lives in a small town, and the cousins, all the same ages, have grown up routinely seeing their grandparents. It's part of their lives. Maddy always had a special relationship with the first-born granddaughter. Amanda rode her bicycle over to her grandparents' house almost every day after school. On the weekends she and Maddy did all sorts of fun things together. Suddenly, when she was twelve, Amanda stopped dropping by for casual visits. "She didn't have time for me anymore," Maddy said. "She had a whole group of friends and after-school activities, and I wasn't so important in her life anymore. It made me very sad, even though I sort of understood." Now Amanda's eighteen and away at school. She and Maddy communicate through their computers. They E-mail each other often and have begun to develop a whole new, adult relationship. "She thinks I'm a pretty cool grandma," Maddy says.

Part of Every Day

Sandy lives on one coast, his grandchild on the other. "Every night before leaving my office, I send my grandson an E-mail message. It may be just a line to tell him I miss him, or it may be a longer message about something I did that day that might interest him. Lately, we've been having an ongoing chess game." he says. "Usually, when I arrive in my office in the morning there's a message back, since he checks for messages before going to bed or first thing in the morning. I feel like he's a part of my day, every day."

 ## By Video

When Jon's son, Stephen, moved halfway across the country, we didn't see his two small children very often. Stephen began taping the kids from time to time, just playing and doing their normal routine. He made duplicate sets of the tape to send to all the grandparents. We in turn circulated the tapes to all the extended family members such as step-sisters, cousins, aunts, great-grandparents, and any other interested parties. The idea caught on, and now everyone tapes milestones and special events to share across the miles. Why not tape a "Day in the Life of Grandma (or Grandpa)" and send it to your grandchildren?

3

Visiting at Their House and Yours

"Nana, I'm so sad," was what I heard on the other end of the phone. "Why is that, Sara?" I asked. "Because I miss you so much and I want you to come to our house right now." Most grandparents would love to drop everything when a grandchild wants to see them.

According to a survey of 45,000 elementary school–age children, if kids were in charge of planning the family vacation, it would be spent at Grandma and Grandpa's house, which tied with Disney World as the destination of choice. Our children and grandchildren visit often. The anticipation is great, but we also have full-time work and have to plan time with them, as do most of the grandparents we know. Preparation is the key to successful visits.

▶ When You Visit Them ◀

When Sandra arrived at her grandchild's house she announced that they were going to see the new Disney movie. "Oh, Daddy and I already saw that," her grand-daughter, Carly, said. Sandra was disappointed because all week she'd been planning to surprise the child with this treat. Daddy said, "Carly, wouldn't you like to see the movie again with Grandma?" But the child was busy playing with her Barbie and didn't respond. Sandra immediately sat down on the floor with the child and said, "That's okay. I'd much rather play Barbies." The child brightened, and Grandma and Carly spent a wonderful hour of quality time together.

Visiting our grandchildren gives us a chance to see them in their environment, and we can enjoy them without upsetting their routine. It's best to go along with whatever they're doing rather than arriving with a predetermined agenda. Small children don't like to make plans way in advance and, if they don't want to adhere to your agenda, this can set up an uncomfortable situation for their parents. Of course, some children are overjoyed with the prospect of a movie, but it's best to check this out with their parents before suggesting it.

How to Guarantee You'll Always Be Welcome

When Richard and Grace visit their grandchildren in the next town, they make a point of staying through one meal only. "Never stay from breakfast through dinner. Always leave while you're still welcome," they recommend. They like that their children tell them their visits are too short. Most grandparents and their children think three days for out-of-town visitors is the limit for three generations to be under one roof and remain on good terms.

Alone Is Better

I love to see my grandchildren without their parents. But this isn't always convenient, since they are too little to travel on their own. So the next best thing is giving their parents time to go off alone, then we plan time alone with the children at their house.

Cross-Country Nana

Nana Sam is an actress in California and has four grand-children, two from each daughter. Until each family moved to Vermont and Florida, she saw them often. "Now I'm a hit-and-run Nana," she says. "I liked it when I could go see them, play with them, and then leave. I do not baby-sit. That is just not my thing."

She admits to accepting only the fun part of her role and refuses to wake up early with screaming children. "Rebecca is the oldest grandchild and the only girl. When she was three we'd go on 'dates' together and do whatever she wanted. We'd eat pizza and ride the carousel nearby. She has a great imagination, and we'd make up stories and act them out." One day Rebecca took Sam to meet the next-door neighbor and said, "This is my nana and she's silly."

This year Sam lost her husband and went to spend Thanksgiving in Florida with Rebecca and her family. "I wasn't feeling all that light and gay," Sam says. Rebecca said, "Nana, when will you be silly?" Sam said, "I'm just not feeling chipper." To which Rebecca replied, "Well, tell me when you're chippy 'cause I want to play." And every day she'd ask, "Are you chippy yet, Nana?" It was hard for Sam to grieve faced with such expectations. She says, "Rebecca takes my sadness away and makes me grateful for today."

Were Our Children as Bright as Our Grandchildren?

While children today seem incredibly bright and terribly worldly, Nana Sam always imagined her role as the trusted sage, imparting wisdom and wit whenever she visited her grandchildren. After a recent visit she had doubts: "Rebecca at three is smarter than me!"

►   **When They Visit You**   ◄

Before your grandchildren arrive, take a tour of your house from their point of view to determine what should be put away. Think of what might be tempting to touch and easily breakable or lost. I have a folk art Chinese checkers board that's usually on the coffee table. After my grandchildren leave I find the little wooden balls under every piece of furniture. Now I try to remember to put it away before they come.

Childproofing Your Home

When our first grandchild was just learning to pull herself up to a standing position by holding onto the leg of a chair or the front of a coffee table, she and her parents came for a visit. We had a large ficus tree in the living room. Before we could notice, she had pulled herself up to the rim of the pot and was scooping handfuls of the dirt into her mouth. Later she opened the doors under the kitchen sink where we kept the cleaning supplies, and when we pulled her away she headed right for the stairs.

That visit made us acutely aware of the dangers that

lurked in our house, just waiting for curious little fingers. The next day, anticipating future visits, we bought covers for the electrical outlets, safety locks for low cabinet doors, and a gate to go across the stairway. We considered taking a course in CPR. A list of emergency numbers is now a prominent feature next to the phone. (See Safety, page 54, for a complete list.)

The Right Stuff

Over the years I've collected all sorts of toys and games from various yard sales, in the attic. I keep laundry baskets filled with toys for different ages. When the kids are coming I bring the baskets out and place them strategically around the house. The baskets provide an easy way to clean up the toys at the end of the day. From time to time I ask my daughters to weed out the toys that are no longer age appropriate, and when their children outgrow a toy they donate it to the cause for younger siblings and cousins. We do the same thing with equipment like strollers, high chairs, portable cribs, and car seats. In this way nobody has to travel with these bulky items. You might add to this a good stock of Barney Band-Aids, which will inevitably be used for real and imagined boo-boos. While we're on the subject, a plastic-lined diaper pail in strategic places is a nice temporary decorating touch.

The Video Store—What's Appropriate, What's Not

Most grandparents I know have taken their grandchildren to the video store at one time or another. Beware! Kids know every video that's been advertised on TV. They are video savvy beyond their years, and yours. If your grandchild's parents haven't briefed you, don't let him get any-thing for which you'll be blamed, no matter how many times he swears it's approved.

Grandma as Teacher

My friend Marlene is a gardening enthusiast. She says, "When I'm with my grandchildren it's so natural for me to teach or instruct them. I have to remind myself that the children really don't care about the Latin names for the flowers. In fact, they can hardly remember the common names when I try to impart this knowledge." One day Mar-lene overheard her granddaughter telling a friend, "My grandma is so smart. She knows the names of every single flower in the universe." This shows that you should keep teaching them what you know. It might prove rewarding in ways you never imagined.

The Well-Stocked Home Office

Since we work at home we have all sorts of office supplies that our grandchildren think are really neat. They especially love to swing around on the swivel chairs and make copies on the copy machine. We clear a desk area for them to use when they visit so that when we are grabbing a few minutes of work here and there (almost impossible), they can do their "work" as well. To create an "office" for your grand-child, set aside an area as his or her work space and consider stocking it with the following items:

- Stack of plain copy paper
- Container such as a coffee can filled with colored pencils (not just crayons, although you can have those as well)

- Electric pencil sharpener (little kids love to sharpen pencils)
- Stapler
- Ruler
- Magnifying glass
- Tape dispenser
- Gum eraser

Small but Necessary Equipment

Our nine-year-old grandson has been testing batteries for his grandfather for five years. This simple little device doesn't cost much, is completely safe, will not cause a shock, and is fascinating to young children. Keep it where he or she can reach it, and have plenty of battery-operated items—such as flashlights, Walkmans, and pencil sharpeners—around that always need testing. You will feel as though you're contributing to your grandchild's scientific education as well.

We also have walkie-talkies at our house. One child goes outside or down to the basement, while the other child goes into a bedroom. They make up all sorts of games that involve "commander-to-central" communications, and one child will take the role of firefighter, police officer, or pilot while the other child is in "distress."

Discount stores sell walkie-talkies and room-to-room intercoms. The kids move the intercoms around the house and plug them in wherever they want to play "office." A calculator is another small and fascinating item they love to use for playing store.

Plan Activities

The biggest outdoor attraction for us is the beach. It doesn't matter what the season; when the kids come, we go to the beach. Even in the winter we bundle everyone up and run on the beach. We always take plastic bags to collect our shells, and when we get home we cover a table with paper and paint the shells. Collecting things from nature, like pinecones in the woods, or picking wildflowers, or collecting berries are things that children love to do when visiting their grandparents. City people can plan other types of simple activities to do when the grandchildren visit, such as going to a park, zoo, or museum. The point is to keep the activity simple and short. If it has an extended value—such as painting the shells or making jam from the berries or creating a wreath from the pinecones— all the better. The collecting is the beginning of the project.

What Comes With Them Goes With Them

When our grandchildren would visit with their parents, I complained about the mess they created. I drove everyone (including myself) crazy, nagging them to pick up their things. Every chair, sofa, and table was covered with stuff. Shoes were always left in the living room. Coats were never hung in the closet, we tripped over toys on the floor, and there were always baby bottles in the sink. The contents of our small house seemed to swell beyond capacity. During one visit Jon turned to me and said, "Remember one thing. What they bring with them goes away with them at the end of the weekend." He put the entire situation in the right perspective, and now I am able to suspend my intolerance and realize that together he and I can put everything back together again in no time, after they leave.

Of course, we usually end up sending them a box of items they forgot to pack, but this is a minor inconvenience.

Forgotten Teddy

After our grandchildren's last visit, I was standing in line at the post office waiting to send the box with the forgotten items. A man stood in front of me holding a forlorn-looking teddy bear. When it was his turn he asked, "What's your fastest service? My grandson left his teddy bear at our house and he won't be able to sleep without it." I guess I'm not the only grandparent sending forgotten items, but my box containing one sneaker, a pajama top, and a pacifier didn't seem quite as important. The next time my grandchildren visit, I will take careful stock of the house, looking under all sofas, chairs, cushions, and beds before they leave. I'd hate to be the cause of a grandchild's sleepless night.

Quality Time for Larger Families

Dan and Joanna raised a large family and now have seven grandchildren all under the age of twelve. "How do you give quality time to each of them?" I asked. Their reply: sleepovers! "When the children are old enough, over the age of two, once a month we have each of them for an overnight. We plan all sorts of fun things to make that child feel special. We sing songs, we read books together, we go to an appropriate event. It's also interesting how this changes the dynamics in their house and enables the parents to pay more attention to the other children when one is away."

Grandchild Abroad

How do grandparents develop a relationship with a grandchild who lives abroad? Carol and Bob have one grandchild. For the first two years of his life he was raised in France, the second two in England. Carol and Bob own two hair salons and work full time. "We take trips to see Mason as often as we can," says Carol, "and in between we have him come here."

Last summer Carol went to Europe and brought Mason back with her for two weeks. His mother and father came for two weeks before taking him home. "So we had him for a month. It was wonderful," says Bob. During that time they held a birthday party for Mason and invited a slew of children. It was a fabulous party, to which all the parents were also invited. "We wanted him to remember his time here, especially since it was the first time he'd been away from his parents," Carol says. Carol and Bob confess that their phone bill looks like the national debt, but they'd rather give up a few luxuries than not talk to their grandchild on a regular basis.

The Grandchild You Rarely See

Kathleen and John had seen their nine-month-old granddaughter only once, when she was three months old. Their son and daughter-in-law were visiting for five days. Kathleen couldn't wait to get her hands on the baby, but when they arrived her mother asked if they might play the baby's Barney tape for her.

"I just wanted to hold her and play with her and get to know her. I didn't think for a minute beforehand that I would have a problem," Kathleen said. "I figured I had three options: One, I could say, 'Gee, I haven't seen her in so long. Could she forgo the videotape for now?' Two, I could say, 'Sure, if you'd like,' and then hold the baby while we watched together. Or three, I could do something else and wait until later to get acquainted with the child."

She opted to watch the video, but the mother held the baby on her lap the entire time. "I guess my daughter-in-law feels uncomfortable with me," she concluded. And from that moment on Kathleen didn't push the issue. Instead she went about her business, always being pleasant to her daughter-in-law. A few days later they were watching television together and suddenly the baby held out her hands toward Kathleen. "It was so sudden and so unexpected that I was taken aback," she said. "But I realized that I had done the right thing, waiting for the child to come to me, never pushing to be accepted." Kathleen says she will call and write to her daughter-in-law more often so they won't be such strangers when she visits the next time. "Who knows? Maybe next time she'll let me have the baby alone for a few hours."

Teaching Values at Your House

Rebecca announced quite unexpectedly to her grandparents that she loves coming to their house for a visit because they leave her alone. Grandma Joan said, "I knew what she meant. We let her loll around in bed in the morning and just hang out with us. We're pretty laid back. We save the Disney trips for her dad. They're often financed by us and she knows they're a gift from us."

During a holiday shopping trip with her dad, Rebecca,

whose parents are divorced, said, "Don't worry about spending too much money, Dad, because Grandma taught me how to shop and spend sensibly." Joan says, "I don't gush over her and I don't spend a lot of money on things, but I'm always direct and I try to instill good values. That's what I have to offer."

Making up a Special Occasion

Since she lives far away from her grandchildren, Sylvia likes to make up special occasions to celebrate with them every time she visits them or they visit her. If it's planting time she says, "Oh good, you're coming for the Daffodil Celebration." They go to the nursery, buy bulbs, and spend time together planting. Or she might say, "Great, did you know it's Craft Week?" and she brings a whole bunch of craft supplies and projects to make. Last year when they visited it was Cookie Contest time, and she had the children making different cookies all weekend. Then she held a contest and invited all her friends in to be the judges. There were blue ribbons and made-up awards. Everyone went home with a bag of cookies.

 Enjoying Everyday Things
Together

I used to try to get all my chores done so when my grandchildren arrived I'd have uninterrupted time for them. Then I learned that the everyday routine things can be fun for kids, especially when you do them together. Before your grandchildren come to visit, don't rack your brain thinking up activities to do with them. Stick to your routine and include them in whatever you're doing. Just alter your chores and errands to be done in short spurts. If you're cooking, include them. If you're gardening, let them help.

Spring Planting

One spring I bought little garden spades for Tori and Tyler to help me fill my window boxes. We dug the holes and one by one filled them with the tiny impatiens from the flats we bought at the nursery. I got a little bit ahead of them, and when I turned around they were picking the heads off all the flowers we had just planted. At times like these, it's best to see the humor in the situation. I then told them we were planting the flowers to make the outside of our house look pretty and we had to leave them so everyone could see the flowers. Still, having them do this with me was a lot of fun and the result was far more amusing than annoying. Next spring, when Cody's old enough to help me plant, I know to tell him the reason we're planting the flowers before we start. Grandchildren teach us as much as we teach them. I silently reminded myself that flowers will bloom again, but if you scold your grandchildren for not doing things exactly right, that's all they'll remember of the experience. Being a cool grandparent takes a lot of patience!

Ongoing Projects

Shallow as it may seem, because we live on an island we become the favorite grandparents in the summer, and our children and grandchildren spend a lot of time here. Two years ago I decided to lay a brick driveway. Before starting I designed a neat, uniform layout. This quickly dissolved into a free-form mosaic when the two-, three-, and four-year-olds decided to help. It became the perfect ongoing summer project, like a giant puzzle we did together whenever they were in the mood. We set up their lemonade stand there, and friends sat on milk cartons while visiting me as I worked with one child or another. From time to time my friend Rosie brought her folding chair and knitting, neighborhood regulars stopped each day to check on the daily progress, and "Nana, let's do bricks" became a familiar phrase whenever a child was bored. I didn't care how long the project took, or how imperfect it looked. Sometimes I worked alone. Sometimes I had this time with only one child. And when things were hectic, three children would be fighting over whose brick went where. The finished driveway is rather interesting. Once in a while, from my kitchen window I see a tourist take a picture of it. I get enormous pleasure when I park the car, and it was amusing for those who watched its progress.

Last year I opened a store, and you can't imagine the endless possibilities for grandkid involvement. While my projects might seem an extreme way to get your grandchildren involved with you, everyone has something, a hobby or career or interest, to draw on for a grandchild's participation. You may be surprised at how receptive they are to learning, if you don't expect too much from them. Grandpa Jake has a classic car he washes and waxes with his grandson, and Grandma Ginny is teaching her six-year-old granddaughter how to make pottery.

Seeing Them Is Enough

It was the weekend after New Year's and we had yet to exchange gifts with our children and grandchildren who live on Cape Cod, just across the water from us. The weather was still mild for January, and we planned to spend the day with Cody and Tyler, ages one and four. On Saturday morning we took the boat over to the Cape. When we arrived two hours later, the snow was coming down fast and furiously even though it had been clear when we left the island. My daughter was waiting to drive us the half hour to their house. When we arrived, our son-in-law Doug was just getting the baby up from his morning nap. Tyler was engrossed in his new video game, and Pop Pop settled next to him on the sofa. While I played with Cody on the floor, Jon, a computer-savvy grandpa, quickly discovered he was no match for a four-year-old. "I feel so bad that we can't go somewhere and do something," my daughter said. "I'm afraid it's going to be a boring day for you, cooped up inside." I assured her that we had come to see the children, and just sitting and watching them play was quite satisfying.

By the time Doug drove us back for the six o'clock ferry, we had: danced with Tyler to tapes of "Here We Go Loop-de-Loo," "Hokey-Pokey," and more; played all sorts of games with each child; read books to the baby; played Scrabble with the adults with Tyler as my "partner" while the baby had his afternoon nap; tromped in the snow; eaten lunch; looked over blueprints for the house they're planning to build; and talked about their vacation plans. We had more fun seeing all of them in their environment than trying to take two little children on an outing.

The next day my friend Rose called to ask about our weekend. She has had similar experiences. "When we go to New York to see Zachary, his parents have a list of suggestions to make our visit more interesting. We have to reassure them that we came to see the baby, not a museum. Doing nothing is plenty."

Outdoor Fun

"Whenever I'm about to do yard work," says Grandpa Frank, "I invite my grandchildren to come over and help." While it takes five times longer than usual to do any project, he says, "The kids love to jump in the leaves after I've raked them neatly into a pile. Then I have them pile the leaves into garbage bags. What normally is a one-hour project usually takes all afternoon." He says it's a great way to give them exercise and an outdoor activity, and to give their parents a little break.

 Baby-Sitting

Most grandparents I know would gladly drop everything to baby-sit their grandchildren, but they can't always get away. Living in another town or across the country presents a logistical problem because of the travel, not to mention work schedules. We live in Massachusetts, and our granddaughters, Julia and Sara, live in New Jersey. It's not so far away that we can't get there, but for us it's a boat or plane trip since Nantucket isn't connected to the mainland. We might as well be in Hong Kong as far as our children are concerned. Usually when they call to ask us to baby-sit it's when they want to go away for a special occasion in the near future.

If time is limited, try to work out a schedule with your children so they get quality baby-sitting time and you get quality grandparenting time. This is easier to do if they live nearby. One of my daughters lives in the same town as her husband's mother. Nana Nancy sets aside one afternoon a week for baby-sitting. She has a crib set up in her workroom for Cody, and my daughter drops him at Nancy's house. My daughter can count on this time for personal appointments like haircuts, doctor's visits, or the gym.

Special Toys at Your House

Andrew and Tori live on Nantucket, which makes it easy to see them for an hour or two regularly. My daughter drops preschooler Tori at our house when she needs time to do errands, and we keep a basket of her toys in her special place for when she comes. These toys never go home with her. They're the toys she plays with only at LaLa and Pop Pop's. Sometimes she brings a friend along, and Tori lets her know the rule: "We have to put everything away before we go home."

Keeping toys in laundry baskets or large baskets with handles makes cleanup easy for young children. Nothing has to be neat and orderly. They just scoop the toys off the floor where they play, and the basket can go into the closet or under a table out of the way until their next visit. Some of my friends have colorful plastic milk cartons for holding toys, and others use large plastic sweater boxes with lids. I found a small doll's crib at the thrift shop, and it's the perfect size for holding all the dolls and stuffed animals we've accumulated for the kids.

The Best Days for Cool Grandparents to Baby-Sit

If your time is limited and you can baby-sit only once in a while, the following days are great times to offer your services, the days when you'll be most appreciated. You will be able to enjoy your grandchild alone and also do something extraspecial for his or her parents. In return, your grand-child's parents will enthusiastically announce, "Guess who's coming to see you?"

- Your children's wedding anniversary
- Either parent's birthday
- Any holiday weekend if they want to get away, such as Memorial Day, July Fourth, or Labor Day
- New Year's Eve
- Any day during a long school break (when parents need a break as well)
- While the parents go to the sleep-deprivation clinic (no comment!)
- When the primary caretaking parent is sick
- When a new baby arrives

Stick to the Schedule, It's Easier

When Tyler was nine months old, his parents went away for the weekend and Jon and I stayed at their house with him. My daughter had written what amounted to book-length notes on his schedule: dos and don'ts, how-tos and how-not-tos, and a million other things. At first Jon and I laughed and tossed them aside. "Does she think we were never parents?" we foolishly remarked to each other once they were out the door. Then Tyler woke up from his nap screaming. "Why is he crying like that?" we asked. I picked him up and tried to console him. He wouldn't stop. "Quick, see if she wrote anything about this," I said to Jon. We grabbed the schedule and found, "When he wakes from his nap he'll be hungry and needs a bottle right away. He's also teething so he may want his Nuk while you're warming it. Check under *warming the bottle* before you put it in the microwave. He'll need a diaper change. But *don't forget he can roll over, so don't leave him on the changing table.*"

From then on we did exactly what was on the list and followed the schedule rigorously, and everything went absolutely smoothly. Remember: If your grandchild's parents take the trouble to write it down, it's probably important. Read it!

Time Stands Still or, Is It Only 10 A.M.?

From the second they awake until bedtime, little children are a full-time, nonstop responsibility. If you've ever baby-sat for a whole day you know how long a day can be. I'm used to taking a little break now and then throughout the day. When I'm working, the time flies. Children go from one activity to the next. Their attention span is short. They are long on energy. They eat lots of meals. They have snacks. By 11 A.M. they've put in the equivalent of a full day's work. Their naptime is always too brief in the scheme of things. I never learn this. Every time I go to baby-sit I bring a book, a project that I must finish, even my laptop computer. Everything goes home with me in the exact state in which it arrived.

The Television Issue

Almost without exception, all my research on grandparenting mentions the television issue. The majority of grandparents think their grandchildren watch too much television. Carol doesn't allow her grandson to turn the TV on in her house. "I make sure we have so much to do there isn't time to watch television," she says. Gary asks his grandson to pick one show during the day that they can watch together. "This gives me a chance to identify with his interests. I like a lot of the shows he watches." But he never lets his grandson watch anything remotely violent.

No Scary Movies

When Grandpa was baby-sitting, Andrew, age ten, wanted to watch the movie *Ghostbusters*. His four-year-old cousin Tyler said, "Me too." Since he had never seen it, Grandpa asked Andrew if it was scary. "Of course not, Grandpa," he answered. Grandpa thought about the difference in the children's ages and, since he was in charge, decided to watch the movie with the kids. He says, "If you let your grandchild watch a video, it should be one that is approved by his parents. You can't always judge what's appropriate and what might be a scary part to a four-year-old." He advises, "Don't just leave him alone to watch something questionable, or you may be the one who gets blamed for his nightmares."

Documenting Your Visit

My daughter and her husband went on a vacation and we took care of three-year-old Sara at her house. During the week we took lots of pictures of all our activities. It snowed and we went sleigh riding and shoveled the driveway. We let Sara take pictures of us sitting on her snow-covered swings and Pop Pop scraping ice off the car. When we got home we made a scrapbook with the pictures and wrote a story called "Nana and Pop Pop Visit Sara." Under each picture was one line that furthered the story. We made up a simple plot line and sent the book to her. This became her nightly bedtime story for a while, and her parents had a record of Sara's week without them.

The Nap Is Your Only Survival Technique

Sam says he's never taken a nap in the middle of the day in his entire adult life, but he advises, "If this is the first time you're left in charge of a toddler, it may be the only way to survive the day. There are twice as many hours in a baby-sitting day than a regular day." There is only one rule in regard to this. He says, "When she goes down, you hit the sack too. Do it immediately. Not after emptying the dishwasher or doing a load of laundry. Trust me on this. If you wait until you're too tired to stand up, you'll miss the opportunity, and your grandchild will get up fresh and new and ready to go again." He adds, "Know that baby-sitting for three days will cost two days in recovery."

Negotiating Bedtime

This is what happens when Ted baby-sits with his seven-year-old granddaughter: Her parents tell him what time to put her to bed. They warn that she'll make all kinds of excuses to stay up past her bedtime, but he shouldn't fall for them. He says okay, he's strong, he can be tough. Bedtime comes and he says, "Time for bed," in his most positive and assertive way. "Please, *please,* Poppy, just one more story and then I promise I'll go to sleep," she purrs while putting her little arms around his neck. "I'm no match for her. I read one more story, sometimes two." He knows he's a pushover but realizes it's only one night out of the year. So while he respects his children's parental rights, he knows as a grandparent he's allowed to bend the rules a little.

Reading a Bedtime Story

Children love repetition and never object to watching the same video or hearing the same story over and over again. They know their favorite books by heart. One grandmother I know loves improvising when reading to her grandchildren, but they always interrupt her with, "That's not the way it goes." Her advice, "Don't get creative. They like it the way it's supposed to be." And another word of advice, "All bedtime stories *must* have happy endings."

All Together at Night

When Rose and Lewis have their granddaughters, Anna and Elizabeth, for the night, the girls bring their sleeping bags, pillows, and favorite blankets, along with their teddy bears. "We make their 'beds' on the floor in Grandma and Grandpa's room for a cozy sleepover," Rose says. "Children shouldn't have to sleep in another part of an unfamiliar house, and this way I don't worry about them getting up at night and falling down the stairs or being afraid. But," she continues, "Grandpa and Grandma have to be prepared to go to bed at eight-thirty!"

Settling Sibling Rivalry

Gabriella came sobbing into the kitchen where her grandparents were having breakfast. Her parents were away for the weekend, and her grandparents had come to stay with her and her little sister. "Lisa ate the last fruit roll-up and you said it was mine and now there isn't another one and it's not fair," she wailed dramatically. "Let's see if we can find something extraspecial for you," Grandma said. Lisa began crying, "I want something special too." "Trying to reason with a two-year-old is not wise," her grandmother said. The solution: Grandpa took Lisa into the other room to distract her with a game while Grandma and Gabriella looked through the pantry for a special treat.

"I'll have the M&M's that Mommy hid on the top shelf," she said, knowing that her parents never allowed candy before dinner. Grandma gave her the candy and said, "You can have this as a very special treat if you save it for dessert and do not eat it in front of your sister." Grandma advises, "Beware, their negotiating skills are finely honed. When you give in, make the terms conditional, yours—or you will forever be in negotiations."

Keeping Them Busy

When Ethan went to baby-sit for his three-year-old granddaughter for an hour, he brought along a roll of colorful stickers to keep the child busy. When her mother returned from her errand she found Grandpa on the sofa covered from head to toe with stickers! This was more fun for the child than simply sticking them to sheets of paper.

If you've had a busy week and you're not particularly full of energy, bring a coloring book and crayons, a roll of stickers, or a new Color Forms set with you for on-the-job distraction. You can relax and participate with your grandchild who will never miss the endless games of hide-and-seek.

Dressing

"Don't you think she needs a sweater?" I ask when visiting my grandchildren. They always seem to be dressed in the most inappropriate clothing. The little girls in particular like to play dress up, and a bathing suit or a ballet costume seems to be the favored articles of clothing in the dead of winter. Why do we always think they need a sweater when we're cold?

Color-Coordinated Isn't the Most Important Thing

One morning Julia presented herself fully dressed in her favorite ruffled pink polka-dot shirt, red plaid flannel pants, orange striped socks, and party shoes. At two she was just learning to dress herself, and she announced, "I ready for cool." We were taking care of her and responsible for driving her to preschool. Could I deliver her in this getup? I wondered. "Julia, you look so pretty," I announced. "I'm so proud of you." She beamed. When I delivered her to the classroom her teacher said, "My, Julia, aren't you looking colorful today." And that was that.

The Snowsuit Maneuver

There's a maneuver that enables little kids to put their jackets on themselves. It seems to have been adopted by preschools across the country many years ago by teachers who couldn't possibly put twenty-three jackets on the kids every time they went out to play. This is how it works:

1. Place your grandchild's jacket on the floor with the inside facing up, with the arms down beside the jacket.

2. The child stands above the jacket at the top so the jacket is upside down facing her.
3. She then puts her arms into the sleeves all the way so her hands come through.
4. She swings the jacket over her head, and it lands on her body.
5. Zip her up.

The next time you say, "Let's get ready to go out," she will know how to do it herself.

Refusal to Dress

Sharon and Pete took care of their twin granddaughters while their parents went away for a week. "The girls know how to dress themselves so don't do it for them," the children's mother said. "Don't let them watch television in their pajamas or they'll refuse to get dressed."

Sharon and Pete thought they could handle this, but the next morning the girls got up and took out their toys. Sharon told them they had to be downstairs for breakfast in ten minutes or they'd be late for school. They ignored her. Then she had an idea. She ran down to the kitchen and brought up the kitchen timer. Setting it to ten minutes she said, "Girls, you have ten minutes to get dressed. Let's see who can beat the timer." Instantly they dropped what they were doing and raced to see who would win.

Naked Is Better

Gloria says her grandson looks like an angel. He has white blond hair, big blue eyes, and a smile that would melt your heart. But he's a terror. He loves to be naked, which is cute, unless it's your job to dress him. Her daughter told her, "Mom, most children his age love to take their clothes off. It's their way of asserting themselves. As soon as they can, they take everything off and run around naked. It's not a big deal." Gloria thought about this as she strapped the child into his car seat, wondering if they'd think it was "no big deal" at his preschool if he arrived naked.

To solve the problem, that evening, just before bath time, she encouraged the child to take off his clothes and to run around naked for a while. While he was in the tub, she told him the story "The Emperor's New Clothes."

"The next day he refused to dress for preschool," she says. "Then I reminded him that he had a special time to be naked, and that time was before his bath or before going to bed. I told him that tonight we would make up a game and pretend that he was the emperor. Then I asked him to show me his favorite clothes. I made up a silly singing game for dressing, and it solved the problem."

One of the great things about being a grandparent is that we are only briefly exposed to common problems like this, whereas our children deal with them daily. We can bask in the illusion that we've successfully solved the problem. However, in reality, the situation has been solved momentarily and will undoubtedly reappear or be replaced by another problem tomorrow. Fortunately, we have the luxury of going home and not always being around to get involved. By the time we see our grandchild again, he may have gone through many different, and sometimes disagreeable, stages. Gloria concludes, "I often go home and dwell on the current problem as I perceived it. When I call my daughter to give her some advice, my grandchild is usually out of that stage and onto something else. Given a little time, most problems seem to disappear by themselves."

And You Thought You Were Physically Fit!

It doesn't matter that you walk three miles every day and lift weights at the gym twice a week. You are no match for the energy of a three-year-old grandchild. No matter how many times we remind ourselves that baby-sitting days are longer than regular days, we seem to forget this between visits. Don't make any plans for the day after you take care of your grandchildren. It will take at least a day to recover, no matter how young and fit you are.

Endless Repetition

Robert does push-ups, sit-ups, and jumping jacks every morning. He plays a strong game of tennis on the weekends. "I thought I was in pretty good shape when we went to visit my daughter's nine-month-old baby," he says. "Janice is just learning to pull herself up in the crib, and when I handed her a rattle she gleefully reached for it. Then she threw it out of the crib. I bent to pick it up and gave it back to her." The baby thought this was a wonderful game. Every time Robert handed her the rattle, she squealed, which gave him great pleasure until he realized there was no end to this game. It would simply go on as long as he could keep it up.

Later he took her for a walk in her stroller. When they started their walk she had a bottle and a pacifier with her. Somewhere along the way he realized they had lost both. He backtracked. He handed her the bottle, holding onto the Nuk. Along the way he got distracted by his thoughts until the baby began to cry. He realized what had happened and again went back for the fallen object. By the time they returned home, he calculated he'd walked no more than three blocks and had bent over more than twenty-nine times. "Next time," he says, "I'm going to tie a string to one end of the pacifier or toy and the other end to the stroller."

The Stroller Situation

While we're on the subject of strollers, Robert adds this, "It's a lot easier to push an expensive stroller with a solid handle that you don't have to bend over to reach, and wheels that don't turn left when you want to go right, than the cheap fold-up kind." His advice, "Provide this item at birth. It will be the best investment you can make until you're called upon to buy her a safe car."

A Day at the Gym

Annette says a day with her grandchild is like spending a day at the gym. "If you're unsure about your physical fitness, consider doing the following to test your durability":

- Carry your grandchild around endlessly, balanced on one hip.
- Bend over to change a diaper.
- Bend over to lift a grandchild from the floor, crib, stroller, or bathtub each time he lifts his tiny hands upward.
- Kneel on hands and knees to wipe up the food that goes from high-chair tray to floor every time he has a meal or snack.
- Sit, lie, kneel, and crawl for all sorts of play activities at which you must excel.

• Take a walk with a toddler, requiring you to bend down to hold the hand of someone who is twenty-four inches tall.

The Preschool Cold

"Why is it," asks Mary, "that preschoolers have colds for four years and we still rush to baby-sit in the misguided belief that we won't catch it?" Staying healthy is a challenge with grandchildren in your life. Many grandparents who never considered it before now get flu shots every year. "I get sick every time I visit them," Mary says. "It never stops me from seeing them. In the winter, I just plan to see them when my schedule is particularly light and I feel rested enough to have the stamina."

The Bath

Vicky says her two-year-old grandson throws a fit every time she announces, "Bathtime." One day she brought along a bag of beach toys, including a watering can, for him to play with in the tub. "I didn't say anything to him as I began to fill the tub with water. The bathroom door was open and he wandered in. I casually kept filling the watering can from the faucet and pouring it into the tub." The toddler came closer to see, then held out his hand to take the object. "Would you like to do this?" she asked. He nodded. "Well, if you stand right here in the water you can fill the watering can and pour the water on your tummy," she said. He allowed her to undress him while he held the toy, and eventually he was sitting in the tub happily playing with the toys and taking his bath.

Vicky was glad to help her daughter-in-law, but the next time she baby-sits she says, "I think I'll arrive after his bath. Holding a baby in the tub, leaning over to wash him, lifting him out, and bending over to dry and dress him is back-breaking work. Did I bathe my children *every* night?" she wondered in amazement.

In the Car

In many parts of the country it is illegal to travel in a car with a child who isn't in a car seat. When our children were little, car seats hadn't been invented. Now our daughters won't turn the motor on until their children are securely in place. For us, this necessitates ownership of this piece of equipment. We have several sizes in our basement for the eventuality of a visit from any family with any age child.

Did you ever lift twenty-four pounds of dead weight, swaddled in a snowsuit, and place it into a car seat? This is a task for the superhuman. Assuming you get your grand-child into the seat without hitting his head on the door frame, you then have to get the strap over his head, another one around his waist, and somehow find the end of the seat belt, which is always too short, and attach it. All this while bending over!

You then make one short stop to pick up a bottle of milk. You must take him out, bend down to hold his hand or carry him, then put him back in the car seat, only to take him out again when you get home. Try doing this two or three times and you'll quickly conclude that children don't really need fresh air. (See *Mayo Clinic Medical Book* for lower back pain.)

Proper Clothing

When Olivia picked up her grandchild and spun her around, the child threw up all over her. She has this advice, "When visiting your grandchildren, never wear cashmere!"

An Hour Is More Like a Day

Mimi doesn't take care of her two granddaughters very often, so when she offered to give her daughter a much-needed day off, Mimi planned all sorts of projects to do with the children. She arrived at nine in the morning. "We made candles from the candle-making kit I brought, we cut pictures from old magazines and pasted them onto pieces of paper to make cards for their parents, we went outside and played on their swing set," she says. "When we came in for lunch I realized it was only eleven. It felt like the day should be over!

"I knew I was in trouble when, after going through my entire repertoire of activities, the littlest one looked up at me with the face of an angel and said, 'What can we do now, Mimi?' When their mother came home she asked the girls what they had done all day. 'Oh, nothing,' was the reply."

Mimi has since learned that it isn't necessary to initiate a bunch of activities so the children are always busy. It's all right to watch them at play with a little interaction. Now she mixes things up a bit so that when they're bored she introduces a project. "I was wearing myself out unnecessarily," she says.

Shopping With or Without Them

If you must take a child shopping with you, know that one errand a day is plenty. Their attention span is about one hundredth of yours. Unless you live in the deep South where snowsuits are unnecessary, if you have more than one child in tow, consider having your groceries delivered during the winter.

Preparing to Go Out in Winter

Taking an infant or small child to the supermarket can involve at least twenty steps before you get there. It's a good idea to be prepared by memorizing the following sequence:

1. Change diaper or put toilet-trained child on potty even against the persistent protest that she doesn't have to go. She always will.
2. Dress the child, complete with shoes and socks.
3. Put on her jacket, hat, and mittens.
4. Pack a bag with an extra diaper, change of clothes, bottle, pacifier, plastic bag, and toy. (Trust me. You will regret leaving any of these items behind, even for a ten-minute errand.)
5. Put the child into the car seat, making sure not to hit her head on the door frame to avoid a hysterical fit before getting started on the outing. Check the seat belt.
6. Put the stroller in the trunk.
7. Drive to the market.
8. Remove the child from the car seat as carefully as she was put in.

9. If there is a strap on the supermarket cart, leave the stroller in the car. If not, take the stroller out before taking your grandchild from the car seat.

10. Go through the market and purchase the items that brought you on this outing as quickly as possible, with no diversions.

11. Reverse the order from 10 through 1 and hope the items in the bag you brought, especially the extra diaper, are not needed before getting home. It's extremely difficult to change a diaper in the backseat of a car.

Buying Diapers

The first time my daughter was coming to visit with our new grandson, she called with a list of items she would need, so I could shop before her arrival. Diapers were at the top of the list. Now, many years later, I know that buying diapers is no simple task. If asked to purchase this item, be sure to ask the following questions to avoid many trips to the store before getting it right: What size? What brand? For toddlers, infants, girls, or boys? Any other relevant information?

Now comes the really important advice: *Never* substitute another brand if the specified item isn't available. Go to as many stores as necessary to get the exact item prescribed. This advice applies in triplicate if asked to buy formula.

Good Things to Avoid

Isabel has this advice when taking a grandchild to the supermarket: "You may never have noticed, but there's a booby trap right by the checkout aisle. While you're busy removing groceries from your cart and piling them onto the moving belt, your grandchild is happily eating through the wrapper on a giant candy bar. They place those shelves of candy within easy of reach of a child sitting in the grocery cart seat."

The only defense is learning exquisite distracting tactics while unloading, like handing the child some of the groceries and keeping up a running conversation with him, even if it's one way and he doesn't understand a word. "You can't imagine the look I got the other day when I asked Joshua if he thought our president was doing a good job. And how about those Packers!"

Buying Baby Food

When Wendy's daughter-in-law asked her to pick up some baby food at the supermarket, she was happy to help. "Only the natural brand, Mom," she warned. But when Wendy got to the store, she was confronted with shelf after shelf of all kinds of baby foods and brands. Reading the labels, she discovered that the discount brand had the same nutritional value as the overpriced natural food brand. Something told her she shouldn't get creative in this area. She bought the brand she was told to get. End of story.

The Supermarket Caper

If you must go to the supermarket with a grandchild in tow, know that you can't whip through in thirty minutes. Allowing small children to be active participants can turn a chore, even a nightmare, into an enjoyable experience for you and the child.

Zanda took her grandson to the supermarket and found,

to her dismay, that he wouldn't stay in the shopping cart. She opened a box of graham crackers to keep him busy. This distracted him for a few minutes. When he fussed some more she took him out of the seat and put him into the cart with the groceries. Then she made a game of having him catch all the soft items like paper towels, napkins, and toilet paper rolls that she gently tossed to him from the shelves.

When Rita takes her three-year-old grandchild shopping, she makes up letter and number games to distract her. As they go up and down the aisles, she says, "How many blue boxes can you count?" Or she asks the child to find a can with a picture of string beans on the label. "Can you tell me if they have applesauce on the shelf?" she might ask. This takes awhile but can be a great way to teach and to turn shopping into a game.

Beatrice took her seven-year-old grandchild to the market and brought along a calculator. Each time she tossed an item into her cart she read the price off to the child, who entered the numbers on the calculator. As they went along, the child kept a running tally, and Grandma said, "I have thirty-six dollars with me. Tell me when we're close."

When they reached the total and had a few more things to buy, Beatrice said, "Now, let's decide what we need most and what we can eliminate. Then they looked at the items and compared prices. In some cases they exchanged a brand-name item for a generic brand and ended up with everything they needed within their budget.

Beatrice reports, "When she said she wanted an overpriced dessert item, I simply told her to figure out how we could buy it by eliminating or substituting something else. We had a really good time comparison shopping, and I felt as though I was teaching her a valuable lesson. Her mother doesn't have time to do this, but I felt good about exposing her to the concept of budgeting."

Safety Is a Priority

Two friends were sipping iced tea after their tennis game. One was about to have her grandchildren for a few days. "We never had to childproof our house when our children were little," Doreen told her friend. "We never had to wear seat belts back in the dark ages either," her friend retorted. "If you want to keep your sanity, put away the Steuben glass."

Essential Safeguards

"If your grandchild is under three years old and about to visit your home, take a trip to your local home center," Laura advises. "They have everything you need to ensure peace of mind and save energy. Without these items you'll be running yourself ragged." They are all inexpensive and simple devices, and you'll wonder how you got along without them when your own children were little. Take this checklist with you:

- Safety plugs for electric outlets
- Gates to put across the bottom and top of your stairs
- Guards to go over corners on tables to avoid an eye mishap
- Rubber pads to go under scatter rugs
- Safety locks for kitchen cabinets that contain cleaning solvents
- Night-light
- Latch to hold down the toilet seat

Taking Your Grandchild in the Car

"Can't you hold him on your lap in the backseat with the seat belt around both of you? The airport is only five minutes from home," I pleaded with my daughter who was flying to the island to see us with our one-year-old grandson. "Mom, we don't go anywhere, not down the driveway, not around the corner to the store, nowhere, if he's not in a car seat. If you want me to bring ours, I will." We bought a car seat, and six grandchildren have made very good use of it.

Note: Always put the child's car seat in the backseat.

Safe Playthings

Before Shelley's crawling grandson comes to visit, she rearranges her accessible kitchen cabinets. "I always equip my lower shelves and drawers with Tupperware, pots and pans, wooden spoons, and anything nonbreakable that he can play with," she says. "He makes a lot of noise, but I don't have to buy a single toy. He has the best time."

The Well-Stocked (and Locked) Medicine Cabinet

Robin reminds us, "I always put together the basic first-aid kit for any eventuality that might occur when my grandchildren visit. One of them always seems to need a Band-Aid or gets a fever in the middle of the night." She suggests adding Barney Band-Aids for real and imagined boo-boos, baby Tylenol, first-aid cream, calamine lotion, bug repellent, and anything else you can think of made especially for children that might not be standard equipment in your medicine cabinet.

Things to Avoid

Dick says his grandson loves it when Dick swings him around in midair while holding onto his ankles. His friend

Don advises him not to do this in front of the child's parents. "And while you're at it, don't take him in the deep end of the pool or throw him into the air no matter how much he loves it. His parents won't."

Good Things to Know

Estelle says, "I never realized all the safety hazards we have to watch for when our grandchildren are coming. I moved all plants from the floor to a higher elevation, removed all the knobs from my stove, taped up a note so I'll remember to put boiling pots on back burners with handles away from the front, locked the tool box, put tape over all the locks on bedroom and bathroom doors, crawled around the floor picking up small pieces of things I can't identify, locked the bar cabinet, put glasses on top shelves, put everything valuable away, removed books from the bottom shelf of the bookcase, rearranged the furniture so the sofa blocks the fireplace, padded the glass coffee table with a strip of foam rubber attached with Velcro—and this is only for the weekend!"

Dangles, Bangles, Buttons, and Bows

If you think your house isn't full of land mines, just count the dangling cords—lamp cords, shade cords, window blind cords, and draw curtain cords. Do

you have a sewing box? A button box? The button box can provide hours of entertainment for any child over four. Under that age, put it away!

4

The Art of Giving Presents

Buying gifts is a grandparent's greatest joy. It's such fun to see their faces light up at the sight of a wrapped gift with their names on it. But buying gifts isn't always easy. If you buy clothes, you have to know what they like and what sizes they wear. If it's a toy, it has to be appropriate for their age group and acceptable by their parents' standards. Buying gifts for grandchildren is an area that can cause conflict between parents and grandparents. Parents often accuse grandparents of overindulgence and spoiling by buying too much, or get annoyed when grandparents buy something the parent feels is inappropriate or promotes the wrong message. What started with innocent, joyful intentions can turn into an unhappy experience.

► What's Appropriate, What's ◄ Not

For one Thanksgiving visit I decided to buy little gifts to place on each child's plate. Because they were all different ages, I wanted to find something appropriate for each one without making too much of the gift or the time to find it. There was, at the time a new product on the market that was a gooey, nondescript substance that felt like sticky Jell-O and could be stretched, molded, and stuck to almost anything. I thought this was perfect. The kids would find it silly. It turned out to be a disaster as it stuck to the tablecloth, clothing, and hair. All the parents, without exception, thought I had lost my mind. It didn't matter that the kids thought I was extremely cool. This was *not* appropriate.

Parents Are the Best Resource

There's nothing worse than watching a child get excited over a wrapped gift only to have the gift itself be disappointing. A good solution is to ask the child's parents what is the best gift to bring or send. They can tell you if your grandchild has any new hobbies, activities, or interests, or if there's anything the child's been asking for.

My daughter, Lisa, is a preschool teacher and author of a delightful children's book, *Island Child*. She started a library for each of her children when they were born. The children have a wonderful collection of classic books, and Lisa keeps us apprised of appropriate new books when we want to give them a gift. We always write a personal message on the title page and sign it with love and the date. It's fun to look back over their books to see how old they were when they read each one. Check with your librarian and local bookstore owner for age-appropriate suggestions.

Small Gifts

Sometimes we want to bring the children something small or have a little gift at our house when they visit but don't want it to be a special-occasion gift. Depending on their ages, sticker books, puzzles and brain teasers, magic tricks, bag of jacks, maze books, Slinkies, kids' magazines, a parent-approved videotape or game are some suggestions.

Gender-Appropriate Gifts

At our house we have dolls, trucks, kitchen sets, and other toys for both sexes. It always amazes us to watch the girls step right over the trucks with absolutely no interest and the boys lose interest in playing with dolls after a minute of curiosity. But it's best not to make assumptions about who will play with what. And it shouldn't matter. If your granddaughter wants a football, and your grandson a baby doll, be the one to provide it, but first ask their parents' permission.

It's the Wrong Message

When Henry, the grandfather of a three-year-old, brought the child a water pistol, the child's father went into a rage. "We don't allow guns of any sort in this house," he stated emphatically. "But it's just a water pistol. It's harmless," Henry said. The child was already aiming it at everything in sight. "Not in this house," the father insisted, yanking the toy away from the little boy, who began to scream, "It's mine! Grandpa gave it to me." Henry argued, "But it's not a gun. It shoots water." "I don't care if it shoots bubbles. It's a gun," his son said.

Henry learned that it's really a good idea to check before giving anything that isn't obvious, and most things aren't. When in doubt, ask yourself, "Does it promote violence in any way?" If the answer is remotely close to a yes, don't get the item. You don't want to send the wrong message.

When in Doubt, Check It Out

When Michael called his grandson, the boy told him about a toy he really wanted. He said his father wouldn't buy it because it was too expensive. Michael wanted desperately to surprise the child with the toy, but he knew better. Instead he consulted with his son and asked if it would be all right to buy the toy or if it would be possible to chip in. His son appreciated the consideration, and together they were able to surprise the boy with a special birthday gift— from his parents and grandparents!

Let Them Try

When Tori couldn't fit the pieces into the puzzle Grandma had just given her, Grandma rushed to her aid. The child immediately lost interest. The next day Grandma sat still, watched, and waited. It was painful watching the child struggle with the problem, but when she finally got each one to fit, both Tori and Grandma were rewarded.

Batteries Included?

Batteries are not included in many toys that require them. If the child opens the box and can't use the toy right away, it will be a most disappointing gift. A cool grandparent always stocks a variety of batteries in all sizes. In fact, one of the all-time best items in the "very small but necessary equipment for the well-stocked grandparent home" category is a battery tester. This can keep visiting grandchildren busy for several hours, provided you have lots of things that run on batteries (see page 25.)

Politically Correct

In my store on Nantucket Island, we sell framed nursery prints from the 1920s. The delightful illustrations are in primary colors, and each one has the rhyme printed at the bottom. They are enormously popular with grandparents and new parents alike. But I often admit to a customer that I find a few of them a little offensive. For example, the last line of "The Old Woman Who Lived in a Shoe" reads, "She whipped them all soundly and sent them to bed." It doesn't seem to bother most people, as they attribute this attitude to another time. However, when sending books to a grandchild it's a good idea to read the book first to see if it sends out an inappropriate message.

Preapproved Gifts

Going with your twelve-year-old granddaughter to get her ears pierced is a gift that must be preapproved no matter how many times she tells you it's okay with Mom. The same goes for pierced earrrings, because it may seem that you're saying it's okay. Other gifts that fall into this category: unapproved CDs, tapes, or videos; violent games or toys of any sort; scuba equipment, a surfboard, skateboard, skis, or any expensive gift you haven't cleared with the child's parents. Don't be the one to introduce your grand-

child to a new adventure like surfing before the parents
have given you the go-ahead.

Pets Are a No-No

Vicky begged and begged to have a puppy for her special
birthday gift when she turned seven. Her parents had always refused for various reasons. When Vicky asked her
grandparents for a puppy, they surprised her with one, creating an impossible situation. If the parents return the dog,
the child will be unhappy. If they don't, there is ill will
between the parents and grandparents. Remember, the pet
will probably be as much work for the parent—if not
more!—as for the child. It's a huge responsibility, and to
be fair to everyone, including the pet, it should be a unanimous decision.

Some parents introduce the concept of taking responsibility for a pet by letting a child have a goldfish, turtle,
gerbil, or guinea pig, which are easier to care for than a
kitten or puppy. Grandparents who want to be involved
might buy the fishbowl with colorful stones and a castle,
or the cage.

The Candy Land Issue

When Sara was three I bought her the game Candy Land.
The box said "for ages 3 to 8." Together we took out all
the pieces. Then we removed the elastic that held the colored cards and lined up the gingerbread men. I asked Sara
to choose one of them: pink, yellow, green, or blue. She
picked up the pink one, looked at it, then put it back. She
did this in turn with the blue, the green, and the yellow.
Suddenly she slid off the bed where we'd set up the game

and said, "I don't want to do this." I asked her why. "Because there aren't any gingerbread girls," she said.

Now she's six. While baby-sitting the other day, I began to tell her this story about when she was three. Halfway through it she interrupted with, "I know, Nana. I still have trouble with Candy Land." I figure her mother is doing an excellent job. Drawing skirts on the gingerbread men or adding tags to the bases didn't make any difference. I may have to write to the makers of Candy Land suggesting they create a gender-equal version of the game.

Cracking the Toy Store Code

George is a seasoned grandparent and has a lot of good advice to offer when it comes to "gift-buying strategies." He says, "First, find a large chain toy store that has the biggest variety of toys. Then walk up and down the aisles until you see the right-age toys, always printed on the boxes. Next, look for advice from a shopper with children.

"When you spot a parent with a child who seems to be the age of your grandchild, ask what would be the politically correct toy for her child. This indicates that you're 'with it.' The parent will know instantly and will tell you, 'They all love such and such.' "

Even if the name of the toy is Pumpkin People and the box contains a bunch of revolting little orange figures, and it costs five times more than you think it should, don't hesitate. Buy it. You will save yourself hours of searching for the perfect gift, guaranteed to be all wrong.

Note: When the recommended age printed on the box suggests three to six, the item is usually more appropriate for a three-year-old than a six-year-old. Grandparents know their grandchildren are smarter than the average kids their age, but the manufacturers don't.

The Spoiling Issue

One of the biggest conflicts that arise between grandparents and their offspring concerns spoiling a grandchild. Grandparents aren't as concerned about the rules. Sometimes spoiling comes in the form of an expensive gift the parents feel is inappropriate. Other times it's allowing a child to stay up past normal bedtime. Although we derive pleasure by spoiling our grandchildren, it's a good idea to know how far we can push the spoil zone so everyone is happy.

Spoiling With Parents' Blessings

We have a penny candy store in our town, and the kids always beg to go there when they come to our house. I used to let them fill a bag with whatever they wanted, until my daughter objected. "She can't have all those sweets at one time," I was admonished. Now I give each child a limit of five pieces according to the mother-grandmother agreement, and only one candy store visit during their stay. Mom and Dad have agreed that the candy store is out of their territory, so it remains my "spoiling zone."

How Much Is Too Much?

"What did you bring me, Grandpa?" is how Taylor greets her grandparents every time they visit. His mother complains, "My parents never come without a gift, and I think this is wrong. She expects it." Grandpa Joe says it gives them pleasure to bring presents to their grandchild.

On one such visit the issue came to a head. Grandpa Joe and Grandma Helen had brought the child a toy her parents felt was too advanced, promoted the wrong message, and was more expensive than anything her parents might buy for her.

Parents today are more enlightened then we are and give more thought to the toys they permit their children to play with. "Our son told us to stop buying anything for his children unless we cleared it with them first," Helen said. "He doesn't want the kids to expect gifts whenever we see them."

Helen tried to explain what pleasure it gave them to bring presents for the children, especially toys that their parents might not be able to afford. "That's the point," their son said. "We don't want the kids to have these things. We're trying to teach our children values."

This is probably one of the most talked about conflicts between parents and grandparents. Educators who have spent years studying the way children play and learn report that children's favorite activities involve things that are not even considered toys.

"We certainly didn't want to alienate our children," Helen says. "So we asked if we couldn't compromise in some way. We don't see the children that often, and we like to bring them gifts when we come." Together the grandparents and parents talked about the kinds of gifts the parents found acceptable. They also made a list of what they considered violent toys or games that promoted the wrong message. "Now, as grandparents, we are much more tuned in and realize what a great opportunity we have to teach something valuable through the gifts we bring."

Only at Your House

Pat and Jill solved the problem of being overindulgent grandparents by having a gift for their grandchildren only when they come to their house for a visit. "When we go to see them, we spend time with them and take walks together or help them ride their bikes," Pat says. "When they come to our house we always have an age-appropriate game for them." Jill goes on, "Then we sit down right away and play the game together and get involved in this activity. As the children settle in we find other things they like to do with us. But when they go home, they leave their games at our house. In this way they have a game they play only at Grandma and Grandpa's house."

► Clothes ◄

Giving clothes to babies is okay because you're really giving a gift to the parents. However, if you want to score with the baby, it's best to bring a rattle or stuffed animal as well. Buying clothes is tricky. If you aren't up on these things, it's impossible to know that T3 means toddler 3 and is quite different from, and often smaller than, a regular 3. When shopping for clothes for your grandchildren it's a good idea to ask their parents beforehand what sizes the children wear in different articles of clothing. One size doesn't always pertain to all items. A child might wear size 3 in a T-shirt but size 4 in pajamas.

Buying Approved Clothing

At Christmastime my daughter directed me to a store frequented by all her friends with preschoolage children. The owner knew the children and their sizes. If this is impossible, ask your children if they have a favorite catalog they might direct you to for buying clothes for your grandchildren.

Clothing Isn't a Cool Gift for Teenagers

Even if your grandchild is a teenager and really into clothes, she has to pick them out herself. My friend Alicia says, "Nothing, absolutely nothing a grandparent buys in the way of clothing for a grandchild will be considered cool." To get around this, Caroline always sends her grandchildren a gift certificate to their favorite store, or a check earmarked for clothing that they can pick out.

More Fun Than Jeans

Last winter I sent five-year-old Sara a pair of pink jeans. Pink is her favorite color. I imagined the mailman bringing my package addressed to her. I imagined her excitement over getting something in the mail. Then I imagined her opening the box, anticipating a new coloring book and crayons or a Barbie doll. At the last minute I tucked a package of pink bubble gum into the pocket. When I called to ask if she liked the jeans she said, "They're terrific Nana"—*terrific* is her new word at the moment—"but I really liked the gum." I was able to be practical and indulgent all in one package, pleasing both mother and child. (Bubble gum in small doses is one of our mother-daughter preapproved items.)

Cool Rule #1. Never give a bathrobe, pajamas, socks, or any other "practical" clothing if it's your only gift.
Cool Rule #2. Buy clothes as nongifts for small children and only the clothes the parents specify. Don't get creative in this area.
Cool Rule #3. Buying party dresses is more fun than underwear, but underwear is more practical and may

be more needed, thus appreciated by the parents. If you buy underwear, also buy a small toy.

Good Intentions

Maddy volunteers at the local hospital thrift shop where she often buys inexpensive used clothing in perfectly good condition. From time to time she is able to find something that she thinks would be just right for one of her six grand-daughters. "The little ones were easily pleased," she says, "but, by the time they were schoolage, forget it. Nothing is ever right. If everyone else isn't wearing it, it's not in style. Most of the time they're polite and don't tell me. One day my daughter said, 'Mom, I know you mean well, but save your money.' That was that. Now I never buy anything they don't specifically ask for."

Never Let Them Know It's Secondhand

When Dee tries to save money by buying her granddaughters used clothing at thrift shops or yard sales, her daughter isn't appreciative. "Mom," she scolds, "I can afford to buy them new clothes, and I won't have my children wearing secondhand clothing." Dee now sends the girls puzzles or coloring books instead. "I send the used clothes to my son for his baby. His wife isn't so critical." And she adds, "Or maybe she's just more polite." When in doubt, send a small check with a note specifying that it should be used to buy something the children need.

Grandpa's Pride

Leon is the only grandfather I know who likes to buy clothes for his granddaughters. He travels often to London where, he claims, they have the most wonderful party dresses just right for little princesses. His daughter says they need so many practical things that it upsets her to see money go to waste like this. "But the girls love getting them and the fancier the better," he says. "I don't care if they play dress up and never actually wear them to a party. I just like buying them. It's worth it to see the look on their faces when they open the boxes." His daughter has come to understand how he feels, and rather than take this joy away she relaxes in the knowledge that all future prom and graduation dresses are taken care of. "And," she grins, "the ultimate surprise will be when he gets the bill for their wedding gowns." Count on it!

Buying Clothes Is a Practiced Art

Terese used to be a buyer in a large department store. She loves to buy clothes for her ten grandchildren and keeps a card in her purse with up-to-date sizes of everything they wear. "I discovered long ago that if you bring a gift of clothing and it's too large or too small, it is a disaster. You have to take it back, then send it to them, and the whole experience of getting the gift is ruined." She also says, "Don't expect your grandchild to be overjoyed when you present him with a big box and he pulls out a sweater or, worse, pajamas. To get around this she often asks, "Is there something you'd really like to wear that you don't have?" She says the kids often call to ask for something new that's beyond their parents' budget, which helps everyone out.

Don't Get Creative

Brenda offers rules for buying grandchildren clothing:

1. Don't make it a gift.
2. Ask their parents what they need, even though this takes some of the fun out of it.
3. Never get creative in this area.

You May Think You're Cool . . .

When Andrew was six we bought him a ski jacket. He thought it was really cool and wore it everywhere. That was four years ago. Recently, Jon and I thought it would be a good idea to get all the grandchildren together on the beach for a photograph. We usually do this for our Christmas card, but this year, with this book in the works, we thought it might be a nice picture to go on the jacket. I put on my favorite capri jeans, the ones that end just above the ankles. In an earlier decade these pants would have been called pedal pushers or, as one of the kids' baby-sitters calls them, my "Annette Funicello look." I think they're pretty cool looking. However, when I met the kids at the beach, Andrew took one look at me and said, "Grandma, what's with the pants?" I knew then that the ski jacket we bought him at age six was probably the last Andrew-approved article of clothing we would ever buy.

The Synthetic Issue

When I asked my daugher what Tori needed for Christmas, she asked me to get pajamas. "Sure," I responded, happy for the suggestion. "They have a real cute nightgown in one of the catalogs." There was a long pause. Then she said, "That's okay, Mom, I'll get the pj's." Was it the suggestion of the nightgown? I wondered. "Is there something wrong?" I asked. "Well," she hesitated, "I only let her wear 100 percent cotton, and there's only one place that carries them." I went to the store she suggested, but they were all out of the cotton pajamas. Since we live in a small town where everyone knows everyone else, the store owner could tell me, "Her other grandma bought the pajamas."

Georgette gives her children money to buy her grandchildren clothes. "It saves a lot of stress," she says. "The grandchildren get exactly what they want, and their parents are grateful."

▶ Sending Gifts Is the Next Best ◀ Thing to Being There

Grandparents often bring gifts when they visit their grandchildren. Those who don't see their grandchildren as often as they'd like send gifts. However, it's hard for a young child to associate the gift with the sender even when his parents say, "Look what came from Grandma and Grandpa." To them it's just a box that came in the mail. Older children appreciate the gesture, though. To make more of a connection between the gift and the sender for the younger kids, Marilyn tries to find gifts that have some meaning in the child's life at that particular time, such as a tutu for a ballet student or a chemistry set for a budding chemist. Then when she calls, or they call to thank her, she can talk about how she can't wait to see a dance recital or to hear about a chemistry experiment. She asked her granddaughter to have Mommy take her picture in the new ballet costume so she could frame it and put it on her desk.

Little Pieces, Assembly Necessary

If I haven't learned another thing about sending presents, I know one thing for sure: Never ever send anything with a million little pieces, and send only gifts that specifically state, "No Assembly Necessary." If assembly is required, don't send it. Or be sure you're around when the gift is opened and be prepared to assemble it as well.

No Strings

When Amy was in college her grandmother sent her a check for her birthday. She had been raised to send thank-you notes and, at the very least, to call when someone sent her a gift. But it was exam time and she was overloaded with work and didn't have time. Feeling a little bit guilty about cashing the check, but needing the money, she found what she thought was the perfect solution. On the back of the check where the line says "endorse here," she wrote, "Thanks Grandma, Love Amy." When her grandmother got her bank statement, along with the canceled check, she laughed and said, "Well, that's a first."

Mary sends her grandchildren gifts even though she gets furious when her daughter-in-law doesn't have them write thank-you notes. "But I try not to say anything," she says. "I just ask if the kids got the presents, but I hate doing that every time I send something."

My mother, who is now a great-grandmother, used to send her grandchildren baked goodies when they were in college. Because she knew she probably wouldn't hear from them right away, she always included a self-addressed postcard with the gift and asked that they just stick it in the mail so she'd know they got the package. Of course, this always encouraged them to write at least a line of thanks and usually a little more.

Rites of Passage

Sometimes meaningful grandchild-grandparent experiences happen by accident. When Alex bought his grandchild her first bicycle, he learned something. The bike was just the beginning. A bike rider needs a patient grandparent to teach her to ride. When she was a few years older, Alex bought her a two-wheeler with training wheels and patiently held onto the seat until she could ride without them. He hopes he'll be around when she's ready for driving lessons.

The Best Gifts Don't Cost a Lot

A gift doesn't have to be expensive to be appreciated. Some of the grandparents I spoke to give their time, introduce new concepts and ideas for growth, and share their experiences that can be far more valuable and lasting than material things.

Gifts of Love

Gifts don't have to be of a material nature. One Christmas, Eleanor's grandmother said, "You have so many toys, sweetheart, and there are lots of children who don't. This year, why don't you pick one of your toys from last Christmas to give to a little girl who doesn't have so much." Together they wrapped the baby doll that Eleanor chose because she said it was almost like new and took it to the fire station where they had set up a collection center. But Eleanor wasn't happy just leaving the present. "I want to give it to a little girl myself," she said. So they asked if this might be arranged. When Eleanor saw the look on the child's face as she opened the present, her grandmother knew it was an experience she and Eleanor would never forget.

Toys From Your Past

Bill and Nancy make all their grandchildren's Christmas gifts. Bill is an expert craftsman with wood. Each year he makes something like a small wooden boat, a pull toy, or rocking horse. When the kids were little, he made wooden blocks of all sizes and shapes for each child and sanded them smooth. They were stored in a burlap bag on which they stenciled the child's name. Nancy makes custom cushions and sails for boats. Last year she made canvas tents for the little boys, and this year Bill and Nancy made old-fashioned horses, the kind with a soft horse head and mane on the end of a long dowel, used for imaginative galloping. Creating old-fashioned toys or games reminiscent of your childhood can be fun for you and your grandchild. Depending on your skills, there are all sorts of ideas and plans in crafts magazines, especially in the November and December issues when people are most likely to make gifts.

Gifts From the Heart

When Rose was about to be a grandmother for the first time, she crocheted a baby blanket. Now there are two more grandchildren, and each has his or her own "Grandma Rose Blanky" that will undoubtedly become an heirloom. My grandchildren all have their own quilts, some made from scraps of their mothers' old clothes. If you don't have a particular needlework skill, consider making a craft item for each grandchild, varying each one slightly so it's unique. This might be a cross-stitch birth sampler, an embroidered baby pillow with a monogram as the design, or a stenciled frame to hold a picture of the newborn baby. There are lots of plans and kits available.

5

Everyone Deserves Respect

A very wise elderly lady once gave me some very wise advice. She said, "If you want to be forever welcome in your grandchildren's homes, never contradict their parents. We may be older and wiser in many ways, but your children know best what's right for their children, no matter how much we may think they don't. Show the utmost respect for your children, and their children will do the same." When my son-in-law is reprimanding his daughter and I want to put my arms out to comfort her, this is very hard advice to remember.

► Your Grandchildren ◄

Joshua collected baseball cards. He complained that his little sister was always getting into them. When he visited his grandparents, Gramps gave him a special wooden box in which to keep them. Together they painted the box and stenciled his name on it. Then they found a secret hiding place that only Joshua and Gramps knew about. Joshua knows his grandpa really understands him because he didn't lecture him about sharing.

Keeping Their Secrets

Clint's grandson often comes over after school, and they do things together. "Whatever I'm doing, he comes along or helps out," Clint says. "Sometimes I'm on my way to do errands, other times I'm working around the house. If I'm at the computer, he either turns on the laptop or does his homework. But our conversations are easy and I know what's happening in his life. I feel lucky that we live near each other."

One day the boy told his grandfather he had a secret he wanted to share. He told Clint he'd overheard his parents talking about a divorce. Clint wasn't sure he wanted to know this, but he was glad the boy confided in him. "He obviously wanted to talk about this to someone he trusted," Clint said. "I promised I wouldn't let his parents know what he'd told me and assured him he could talk to me anytime he wanted. There wasn't much I could do to reassure him about his parents, but I was a divorced father so I could tell him that both his parents loved him and that I knew it would all work out for the best." Sometimes, in times of crises, grandparents can be a great comfort to their grandchildren.

No Words Necessary

Boris and Greta were in the park with their grandchild when a stranger bent down and asked the child, "How old are you, sonny?" In unison his grandparents said, "Three," just as the child thrust his hand forward holding up three fingers. "My, my, what smart grandparents you have," the man said, patting the child on the head. "Next time someone asks our grandchild a question," says Greta, "I know to count to ten and give him a chance to speak for himself, even if it's sign language."

Developing Trust

My friend Rose, a child development specialist, says, "I have a shelf in my home office where Elizabeth and Anna keep the toys I've given them. Every time they come to visit they go right to the shelf. I never touch anything on that shelf, so it is always just the way they left it. This year Elizabeth, the six-year-old, gave me two of her brand-new Raccoon Beanie Babies to keep in her special place. Children develop trust for their grandparents in these small ways."

She goes on to say, "Whenever Lewis and I baby-sit, we take the girls for a walk. The teacher in me likes to promote developmental skills, and my favorite at their ages is called sorting and classifying. Children like to collect and put things in order. As we walk we collect rocks, sticks, leaves, and berries. When we get home they have a lot of fun sorting out their collection and putting their things in a special box called 'Important Things.' When they go home, the box stays on their special shelf. Every time they visit we add to the collection. Their box of things is always right where they left it. Nothing ever gets moved or thrown away."

 ## Their Parents

Never forget this golden rule: Your grandchildren's parents have the last word.

Bedtime

When Jordie's grandparents were visiting and his parents said, "Jordie it's time for bed. Say good night to Grandma and Grandpa," they didn't say, "Does he have to?"

Dangers Real and Imagined

Respectful grandparents never take their grandchildren on a boat, on a motorcycle, in a sportscar, in a private airplane, or anything else that would make their parents nervous, unless they have permission to do so.

 ## Their Imaginary Friends

Jon and I are quite familiar with the personality traits, likes, and dislikes of Sara's and Tori's imaginary friends and find these little friends quite enjoyable, even when they sometimes misbehave.

We never make the unforgivable mistake of sitting on "Twinkle." When an accident occurs we know exactly whom to blame.

We know that Twinkle does all the misbehaving, but we're careful to tell Sara that she must teach Twinkle good manners.

We always include "Becky" in all our outings with Tori,

as well as in all conversations. We are always respectful of Becky's feelings and treat her with consideration.

When Tori doesn't want to take a bath or pick up her toys, we say, "Why don't you and Becky take a bath togther." Or, "Can you show Becky how to pick up your toys?"

When I was a child I had an imaginary playmate named "Coco." From time to time my mother still sends me articles from her local paper about imaginary friends. The most recent one, written by a child psychologist, explained that children who have imaginary friends are intelligent self-starters. It went on to say they will grow up to be independent people. I don't know about the psychological aspects of this relationship, but I do know it's a great way to teach children all sorts of things like good manners and how to do chores, and to get them to eat their meals by simply saying, "I think Twinkle is hungry now." Or, "Let's teach Becky how to brush her teeth."

▶ Different Religious Beliefs ◀

The Jewish holidays were coming up, and Wilma was excited about introducing her grandchildren to the rituals. She was concerned, however, because her son-in-law was of another faith. "A friend in the same situation suggested I tell my daughter and son-in-law my plans and invite the other grandparents as well," she said. She then called her son-in-law and said, "I have no intention of pushing our faith on your children, but I'd like them to know about our family's heritage." This turned out to be a joyous time for everyone, and now the children brag about how they get to celebrate both Hanukkah and Christmas. Their friends are envious, thinking only about the double amount of presents they receive.

Wilma says, "When we went to our children's house for

Christmas dinner our grandchildren asked if we had a Christmas present for them. I reminded them that Grandpa and Grandma are Jewish and that we already gave them a Hanukkah present."

Both sides of the family acknowledge the holidays of both religions, getting together with one set of grandparents or the other, and feel the children are getting a well-rounded education. Wilma says, "At first I was tempted to ask questions about how they were planning to handle the issue of religion. Fortunately, good judgment got the better of me and I decided not to meddle in my grandchildren's religious upbringing. I feel parents have the right to make these choices, and by respecting them I'll steer clear of a mess of conflicts."

Religion Can Be a Touchy Subject

Rosalind's grandchildren have divorced parents. Their mother is Catholic and their father, Rosalind's son, is Jewish. When the children came to visit with their father during their Christmas holiday, Jacqueline, the seven-year-old, showed her grandparents the gift she'd received from her mother, a gold cross that she wore on a chain around her neck. Rosalind and Frank were upset, thinking this was an out-and-out insult and the children's mother was letting them know how the children would be raised in regard to religion. Their son didn't seem perplexed by this.

"I see that the children are learning about their Christian background," Rosalind said to her son. "Do you mind if I tell them about their Jewish heritage?" With their parents' blessing, Rosalind began what would become, over the years, an ongoing and fascinating story that included the history of their great and great-great-grandparents. Rosalind says, "Rather than be upset, I realized if I could make it interesting for them, this was an opportunity for me to teach them some of the things I think they should grow up knowing about our side of the family.''

 # Other People

Granny and Gramp took Rasheed to the playground, where the child stood staring at a couple sitting on a bench. They were speaking in sign language, and the child was fascinated. "What are they doing?" he asked his grandparents. Granny and Gramp used this opportunity to teach the child respect for those with a handicap.

After the playground they went to the library to get a book on sign language. Together they perfected a few words, and Rasheed thought this was a wonderful new game. At the end of the day, when his mother came to get him, Rasheed turned to Granny and Gramp, put a finger to his eye, then put his hand over his heart, then pointed to each of them, signing "I love you."

Diplomatic Grandma

Christopher looked up at Nana Flo and in all innocence announced, "You're fat." His mother was horrified and embarrassed for her mother-in-law. But Flo was quick to answer, "Isn't it wonderful that he's aware that people come in different sizes?" putting everyone at ease. His mother didn't have to cut in with a critical, "Mind your manners." When Nana left, Mommy was able to talk to her son about things that can hurt people's feelings.

► **Giving Advice**

When etiquette expert Judith Martin, aka Miss Manners, was asked how grandparents should handle their disapproval of the way their grandchildren were being raised, she said, "Hands off." Arthur Kornhaber, child psychologist and head of the Foundation for Grandparenting, disagrees. He thinks issues should be discussed. "Grandchildren have to understand that Mom and Dad and Grandma and Grandpa don't have to agree on everything," he stated in a recent interview. "Conflict is normal, problems are normal, emotions are normal. You may have a fight, but if you're committed to each other, you come out the other end. It's great modeling for the kids."

I asked a few parents and grandparents what they thought of this, and I tend to agree with the consensus. All agreed that grandkids don't need to be raised by two generations, especially adults who get worked up into a fight over issues. The grandparents already raised their children and aren't involved with day-to-day problems of raising their grandchildren, nor do they want to be. Most grandparents take a hands-off approach when it comes to important behavioral situations. They know it's better for the parents to handle it and prefer a loving, accepting, and supportive role in their grandchildren's upbringing.

New Parents Are Vulnerable

Clarissa says, "When my children were little my mother bombarded me with articles she'd clipped from her local paper or from magazines about child rearing. It made me furious. I wondered if she was sending me messages that I didn't know how to handle situations. Now that I'm a grandmother she still sends articles, only now they're about how to be a good grandmother!" Clarissa's daughter just had her first baby. Clarissa has vowed never to send her daughter articles but remembers to tell her what a great job of mothering she's doing every time she sees her. "This doesn't mean I don't clip the articles," she says. "I just don't send them. I have a big file drawer and maybe some day she'll snoop through it and find something she can use."

Giving Advice When Asked

Alice has three daughters-in-law. "Now and then I'd send them an article I came across about raising children. I began to sense resentment, as if I were criticizing their parenting skills. Now I wait for them to ask for advice about something, and I say, 'You know, it's been a long time since I had kids, and parents today know so much more than we did. But I've heard that some parents try . . . ' and then I go on to give them some advice I've read about. They seem to respond more favorably."

A grandmother of three says she's always more careful when giving advise to her daughter-in-law than her daughter. When I asked why, she said their relationship is too new and she hasn't had the time to become as intimate as she is with her own daughter. I asked what she does when her daughter-in-law asks for advice. "She doesn't, and I'm careful not to offer unsolicited advice."

Grandma's a Pro

As a family therapist, Natalie says when she goes to see her grandchild she often cringes at the way her children, as parents, handle problems. "It's tempting to leave books open to the page that addresses a specific problem. Fortunately, good sense takes over at the right moment and I restrain myself," she says. Her children and grandchildren love to see her and think she's the most accepting and accessible person they know.

When in Doubt, Don't

"Every time I read something about sudden crib death syndrome, random kidnappings, toys that are hazardous, or behavior disorders, I call my daughter immediately to report on these possible mishaps, half expecting to find I'm too late," Linda says. "Fortunately, I count to ten, ask how everybody is doing, and almost always hear about the baby's wonderful new accomplishment. In the face of such news, how can I possibly ask if she's checked to see if the child is still breathing?" Linda expects to get over this by the time her grandchild goes to college. We expect not.

The Food Issue

When trying to get little Betsy to eat her lunch, Grandma Tess learned a valuable lesson: "If you want to get a child to eat something, never tell her it's good for her."

Time Out for New Parents

"My grandchild's parents were walking zombies for months after the baby was born," says Jonelle. "I arrived just in time to give them a much-needed break." However, when Jonelle's daughter-in-law told her the three-month-old baby woke every two hours screaming to be fed, all through the night, she was shocked. This was not a premature baby. This was a healthy, chunky, well-nourished baby who had gotten used to feeding on demand. "Did you know that most babies are sleeping through the night at this age?" she wanted to say but didn't.

Jonelle suggested they wheel the baby's bassinet into her room, far enough away from his parents so he wouldn't be heard. His mother was reluctant, but finally exhaustion won out. "I knew this baby was well fed and in no danger, so I allowed him to cry when he woke the first time," she says. "I admit, it was horrible. I patted his back, but I did not pick him up." When he woke an hour later she fed, burped, and changed him, then put him back to sleep. "He whimpered a little but fell asleep."

Two hours later, right on cue, he woke screaming again. This time she let him cry himself back to sleep. This continued through the night, and each time Jonelle helped him wait a little longer between feedings. By morning she was dead tired, but she kept this up, using common sense all through the day, the next night, and the next day. By the time she went home three days later the baby was on a better routine and on his way to a more normal schedule. Jonelle's children couldn't thank her enough, and when she left they said, "I can't imagine why he sleeps for you and not us." Now they want to know when she can come back to get him to sleep through the night. "First," she says, "I need a month to catch up on my sleep."

Unconditional Love

Hannah, a day care director and grandmother of many, knows a great deal about young children's achievements. "If I've learned anything, it's this," she says. "When my grandchildren aren't living up to prescribed accomplishments for their ages, the solution is simple. I lower my expectations." They all know they are loved, unconditionally.

Keeping Abreast of Changing Trends

"As grandparents, it's tempting to give our children advice on parenting," Sean says. "But if you start sentences with words like 'When you were little we always . . . ' whatever follows will be tuned out." He goes on to advise, "We did things a long time ago, under different circumstances. There's a new way to do everything. There are new rules for every situation, and there's a new baby guru for every generation. If you want to be listened to, don't quote Dr. Spock, unless he's the guru of choice. Get with the new program so you can really get involved discussing real issues as they arise in real time." Musing about this, he made a mental note never to start sentences with any of the following as well: "Shouldn't you . . ." "Why do you . . ." "Won't he . . ." or "We never did that with you."

Developing Independence

Jared says it bothers him when his daughter asks his grandson if he's ready for bed. "Since when do you ask a three-year-old if he's ready for bed?" he asked his wife, Marjory. "Or, 'Are you hungry?' Don't they know about rules and schedules? When it's bedtime, it's bedtime, and when dinner's served it's suppertime, and that's that."

Marjory is a bit more understanding. She said, "They're trying to make him independent and teach him to make choices for himself. Today's children are being taught to speak up for themselves." She remembers when her own daughters were little and she would foolishly ask, "Would anyone like to do the dishes?" Well, she has to admit, it certainly made them independent.

Grandparents as Parents

Some grandparents find themselves in the untraditional role of sole caretaker of their grandchildren. Corita, a wise grandmother in this position at an age younger than she had imagined, says, "While not by choice, I took on this role, accept it gracefully, give as much quality time as possible, and combine that special grandparent love with all my other responsibilities."

The Fold-Out Photo Album

Valerie's paddle tennis group is made up of grandparents. They have an unwritten law that allows for a certain amount of tolerance when talking to one another about their grandchildren. Everyone gets equal time. "However," she advises, "if you want to keep your friends, know their limit. Never brag to the point of becoming obnoxious, never drag out more than one or two photographs, never show an after-dinner slide show or videotape of your granddaughter's ballet recital, and keep the cute quotes to a minimum."

When to Say Nothing

Grandma Bridget says she could have bitten her tongue the other day when her daughter was getting her grandchild ready to go to the playground. "Doesn't he need a sweater?" she asked, as if her daughter didn't have the brains to know this. "I can't imagine how I get through a day without you," her daughter chirped with good-natured sarcasm.

Bridget says she should have known better but is convinced that her grandchild must always be cold. "At least I didn't suggest this might be the reason her nose is always running from here to New Jersey," she adds.

 ## The Fine Art of Praise

I learned a great lesson from a friend who became a grandparent before I did. She said, "If you love seeing your grandchildren—and who doesn't?—you will ensure that they come often if you always praise their parents for doing a great job. When the toddler stands at the top of the slide, for example, it's best not to scream, 'She'll fall if she doesn't hold on.' Instead, you might say, 'It's so nice that you're encouraging her to be so fearless.' "

Praise for the Juggling Act

Although many grandmothers are now working, they may not have been working back when they were raising children. Sometimes it's hard for grandmothers to get used to the idea of grandchildren growing up in a two-career family.

However, Syndey, grandmother of four, all with working mothers, says, "It's important to recognize the changes that we ourselves helped bring about to further the rights of women in this country. Sometimes, when I call in the afternoon and get the baby-sitter, I feel sad, but I would never say this to my daughter or daughter-in-law."

Instead she tells each mother of her grandchildren, in all sincerity, "I honestly don't know how you juggle child care and work and do it so well." She adds, "Even if the sink is piled with dirty dishes, I just remind myself that raising and supporting and educating children today is a lot harder than when we raised our children."

Praise Takes Practice

Carol's daughter-in-law told her, "Please don't tell Billy he's such a good boy. You're putting the emphasis on him rather than what he did. I'd prefer it if you told him you like the way he put his toys away." Carol decided this wasn't a good time to ask how his toilet training was progressing.

Grandma Ginny says that after six grandchildren she finally has her praising skills down to a fine art. Unlike her friend Carol, she knows enough not to say, "You're such a good boy," when three-year-old Christopher does something he was told to do. "Oh, no," she says, "I always say, 'I like the way you did that.' " Her daughter thinks she's well on her way to becoming a politically correct granny.

Sincere Praise

Roberta stated emphatically, "My grandchildren are all geniuses." Grandpa Henry says, "If she said they're bright children she might have more credibility. Then again, all grandparents in our group think their grandchildren are superbright, superclever, inordinately witty, and talented beyond belief! And you know what? They sincerely believe it."

 ## All Grandchildren Are Created Equal

"All grandchildren are created equal," said my husband's grandmother, "except mine. They're smarter, more beautiful, and more talented than anyone else's grandchildren." When a first grandchild arrives, we think there was never a more perfect baby, including our own. We wonder if any child can be as special as that very first one. As each new grandchild comes into our lives, we discover that all grandchildren are equally loved and just as special as the first one.

Always the Favorite

I was fortunate to have a grandmother until I was grown and had children of my own. All my life, whenever I called my grandmother, her response to my voice was, "I'm sooo glad it's you. I was just thinking about you." Or, "Oh, my favorite grandchild. I'm sooo happy to hear your voice." I don't know if she responded to my sister or my cousins in the same way, but I do know that I do the same thing with my grandchildren, no matter which one calls.

There's No Such Thing as an Innocent Question

Sometimes it happens. We ask an innocent question of a grandchild's parents, like, "Why isn't he walking yet?" and we're met with a variety of emotions. A daughter-in-law may never speak to you again. Your son might shrug it off. No question about our grandchild's inability to do anything is acceptable.

No Comparison

The urge may come over you to compare children, especially when it comes to achievement, but this is totally uncool. An innocent question like, "Your sister's baby is already speaking in sentences. When do you think he'll say something?" doesn't deserve an answer.

You Can't Overpraise

When Jon and I got married he had three sons and I had three daughters. But more than that, he had a very large extended family including many cousins. My new mother-in-law, the oldest of five girls, was the matriarch of the family and the person through which all family news circulated. In all the years I knew her she never had a critical word to say about any family member, which included new in-laws, ex-in-laws, children, grandchildren, and step-grandchildren. If you were related in the remotest way, all your accomplishments great and small were celebrated through the family telephone lines. But above all her grandchildren were the most talented, the best looking, and the brightest in the world. If she talked about one child's accomplishment it was quickly followed by a list of something good about each and every one of the others. It was a wonderful trait, and she was loved and admired by every single member of the family until her death at ninety-six.

One-on-One

Jon's mother did do one thing that wasn't quite as cool as I made her out to be. Whenever an out-of-town family planned a visit, she immediately got on the phone to each and every in-town relative to invite them for dinner at the same time. This was her way of getting everyone in touch with everyone else, but it prevented her from enjoying a one-on-one relationship with the visiting grandchildren.

One of Jon's sons lives far away, and when he visits his mother and stepfather with his wife and two small children they usually arrive to a houseful of his brothers, stepsister, extended family, and children all eager to see them. His mother complains that she doesn't have enough time to get to know his children. I don't know of a perfect solution, but if this is your situation, it might be worth discussing it with your children to see what they suggest.

A Word to the Wise

When Beth's daughter breast-fed her first child, Beth said "Breast-fed babies have an advantage. They grow up to be healthy, happy, and smart." When Beth's daughter-in-law bottle-fed her first baby, Beth announced, "Bottle-fed babies grow up to be healthy, happy, and smart." She is equally welcome in both households, and both her daughter and daughter-in-law think she's pretty cool.

How to Display Family Photographs

When our first grandchild was born, we took lots of photographs. By the time we had five grandchildren, there were obvious gaps of missed photo opportunities. We decided to create a photo wall in our studio. Only one family at a time would fill the wall completely, and we changed the selection prior to each different family's visit. This worked two or three times until we forgot to change the photographs between visits.

If you have more than one grandchild, there is no fair way to display photographs, unless you do as my friend Rose does. She has four children and three grandchildren, and every surface of her tables and walls is covered with every family member's progress from birth to the present with all their childhood artwork framed as well.

I have discovered that children count how many photographs of each grandchild you have displayed. If one child is overexposed, you will surely be charged with the ultimate grandparent sin of favoring one grandchild over another. It's a no-win situation and one to take very seriously when mounting your exhibit. The same advice applies to photos on the fridge and carrying photographs in your wallet—all or none.

Out-of-Town Grandchild

Making the out-of-town grandchildren feel just as special as the grandchildren who live nearby is a balancing act. On a rare Thanksgiving visit Susie told her grandchild, "Spending time with you is so special because I don't see you often enough." She always has something special to do with only that child when she comes so they will have quality time together. "When I talk to her on the phone I mention something about what we did together. This helps to keep our relationship alive," she says. "Of course, I have to be careful to plan things when the other children are occupied, to avoid any jealousy," she adds.

You Can't Always Expect a Hug

Betty and Dick are not as close to their son Richard's children as their daughter Betsy's children. "We're a big, loving family," Dick explains, "but our daughter-in-law's family is more reserved. She isn't comfortable with our open show of affection. When we all get together for a family holiday, Betsy's kids run and jump on us and give hugs and kisses. We try to give the other children the same kind of attention, but they won't let us kiss them and push away when we try to hug them. We've learned not to expect kisses from them, as their mother says she doesn't want them to feel they have to let adults touch them when they don't want to be touched."

Betty and Dick find that, while it's hard to kiss some of the children and not the others, they have to respect their daughter-in-law's wishes and those of their grandchildren. But this doesn't prevent them from giving all the children equal attention and looking for other ways to involve their son's children.

Betty remembers one particular Christmas, when both families were together, she was taking something out of the oven when one of Richard's little girls came over and hugged her, then ran off to play with her cousins. "It was most unexpected," Betty said. "But I didn't make anything of it and just assumed she felt comfortable enough, at that moment, to hug me in a casual way. It was as if the environment we created in our household had finally rubbed off on her. It may not happen again, but I will accept what comes my way and continue to love and accept them all equally. Who knows? Maybe someday I'll get a kiss from her brother."

6

Rules for Behavior

"I can do anything I want in Nana's house," Sara told her mother when doing something her mother told her not to do. "Right, Nana?" she said, turning to me for confirmation. When she was little and asked if she could jump on my bed, I said, "Sara, you can do anything in Nana's house." She used to find all sorts of things to confirm this over and over, like having two cookies instead of one, or staying up past her bedtime when she slept over. But nothing she did crossed the boundaries of what her parents considered good behavior or acceptability. However, now she's six and her parents don't think this is so cute. They want her to behave according to their rules about good behavior, no matter where she is. We've since had to revise this rule to, "You can do anything in Nana's house as long as it's all right with your parents."

My daughters recognize the fact that it's fun for kids to get away with things at their grandparents' house that they can't at home. And relaxing the rules for a few days won't negate the good stuff they're trying to instill. They also know that it's fun for us to be the good guys, or pushovers, because it's only temporary. This is one of those small grandparent perks.

We may think it's cool to drop the rules, but it's not if we alienate our grandchildren's parents. Now we are trying to reestablish the rules. With her parents' help, I have to find things she can do only at my house but that are acceptable to her parents as well. This is ongoing, because the kids are in a different stage every time we see them. As parents and grandparents we have to keep reinventing ourselves. It can be an interesting challenge.

 ## Respecting Their Rules

A word from a wise grandpa: "It doesn't matter how much your grandchild begs and begs you to let him do something his parents said he couldn't do. Don't let him do it. If you do, the next time you want to see your grandchild, his parents will be less than enthusiastic."

Parents Have the Last Word

When our son-in-law felt it was necessary to discipline his four-year-old, he took her into the next room to give her time out. She cried and screamed for me to come rescue her. It broke my heart, and it was all I could do not to respond. I appealed to her father, who refused to let me go into the room until the five minutes were up. It was pure torture until she broke us all up by yelling, "Nana, do something bad so he'll give you time out and you can come in here with me." Your grandchild's parents always have the last word. Period. There is no rationale for it being any other way no matter how difficult this seems at times.

His Mother Doesn't Think It's Cute

Celia's six-month-old grandson, Charlie, had just been introduced to solid foods. Celia loved feeding him. "Every time I put a spoonful of cereal into his mouth he'd spit it out," she said. "I couldn't help laughing because he was so cute. Of course this encouraged him to keep doing it. When my daughter saw this, she gave me a long lecture about the seriousness of developing good eating habits." Now when Celia visits she's careful to defer to the way her daughter wants things done, but she says it isn't as much fun.

Sometimes our children seem terribly serious about child rearing and we want to tell them to lighten up. But it's better to respect the fact that they're learning to be good parents, and once they're more comfortable in their role they'll be able to relax. Be patient. This often doesn't happen until they have a second child.

Too Many Sweets at Grandma's House

"When my daughter, Ellen, scolded me for giving my grandson too many sweets," Grace says, "I told her I was sure two Oreos wouldn't kill him."
She goes on to say, "Fortunately this was not my daughter-in-law, because she never would have said what my daughter said next. She said, 'No, Mom, it won't kill him. But I don't want him to have chocolate before going to bed, so why is it so important to you that he does?'" Grace continues, "She put me right in my place. At first I was defensive, then I was grateful. My daughter-in-law might have been

more polite on the surface and then complained later to my son, causing tension in our relationships."

"You're right," Grace told her daugher. "It's not easy learning to be a grandparent, and I'm glad you're helping me ease into this new role." Then she asked if there was any way she could spoil her grandson without upsetting her daughter and together they're working on this and a lot of other areas of grandparenting. Grace wisely concludes, "It's so easy to get angry and defensive, but so much more satisfying to work through these things together. The important thing is, they're living with your grandchildren every day and responsible for them every minute. We get the icing on the cake, so why abuse the privilege?"

Your Grandchild Thinks You're Cool,
His Parents Don't

Every time eight-year-old Jackson goes home after a visit with his grandfather, he brags to his parents about the things Granddad lets him do. "He's so cool," he told his father after Granddad let him steer the car around a parking lot. Jackson's dad didn't think this was at all cool and let his father know it. "But the boy is just having a little harmless fun," Granddad said. "It's against the law, I don't think it's safe, and I'd rather you didn't do it," the son told his dad.

It was fun having his grandson think he was cool, but Granddad knew he'd have to be cool in a more parent-acceptable way. He's currently learning to rollerblade.

Making Rules in Your House

There are things that children are allowed to do in their own homes but that drive grandparents crazy when they do them at their house. Jake won't let his grandchildren eat dinner in front of the television set in his house even if they do it at home. Sheila's grandchildren have to finish everything on their plates or they can't have dessert when they come to her house. Clara expects good manners when her grandchildren are at her home. "I'm a little stricter about this than their parents, but they don't seem to mind when I remind them not to talk with food in their mouths and things like that." You *can* have rules in your home that the children don't have to follow in theirs.

In Praise of Parents

Jon and I think all our kids are doing a great job raising their children. We have a lot of respect for them and think they're all good parents. Our style of parenting was different from theirs, but we try to be supportive.

Recognizing this, one day I was complimenting my daughter on how she allowed two-year-old Julia her feistiness. Suddenly the child was standing on the kitchen counter and I wanted to scream, "Get her down from there, she'll break her neck." Instead I said, "Look at how agile that child is. And so independent!"

Later I looked into the dining room and saw her sitting on top of the table where they keep the gerbil cage. Julia had lifted the gerbil from its cage and was swinging it by the end of its tail. All I knew at that moment was, if she drops that furry thing and it gets lost in the heat ducts I will never again sleep in this house. But I managed to collect myself and, wanting to continue complimenting her, I calmly said, "Julia, it's so nice that you love animals, but Delphine looks very thirsty so I think you should put her back in the cage, sweetheart." My composure was short-lived, however. When this same child took bites of red licorice and lined them up on my white sofa, I totally lost my cool. Our patience is always being tested, but we keep working at it.

Interior Decorating

Totally cool grandparents do not have white sofas.

Relaxing the Rules

When our grandchildren visit, I tend to relax the rules. Okay, I admit it, sometimes I ignore the rules. After all, I didn't make them up, so it's easier not to enforce them. Besides, no grandparent wants to be the heavy.

The children know where the cookie drawer is, and they often help themselves without asking. They walk around the house eating, and my attitude is, when they leave I'll clean up. Their parents, on the other hand, are much stricter and don't want them to eat between meals and then only in the kitchen. I try to respect their wishes, but the kids are usually persistent and I give in. This is one of those things we've talked about, and both parents and Grandma have decided it doesn't happen very often and it's okay for the kids to feel they're getting away with something so trivial.

Hearing Both Sides

On the other hand, Frank says, "When my grandson comes to visit he loves to ride on the tractor with me, but his parents don't think he's old enough and have stated quite firmly that he isn't to do this. Do they really believe I'd let anything happen to him?"

Shirley, his daughter says, "Of course my father wouldn't intentionally let anything happen, but if I'm worried about my child's safety then I can't enjoy being with my parents. I've explained this to my dad and even said that I might seem irrational, but I can't help how I feel, so this is how it has to be. Fortunately, he understands. Maybe next year, but for now Dad's bought him a toy tractor and everyone's happy." Frank says, "In the end, it's best to listen to the parents, even if you think they're being unreasonable. If you don't make a big deal out of it, they may see things your way, when you least expect it. Sometimes they even think it was their idea!"

Their Way Isn't Always Best

When Nana Sam agreed to baby-sit for her two-year-old granddaughter, her daughter emphatically said, "No matter how hard she cries, do not give her a bottle. We are trying to wean her, and I want you to let her cry herself to sleep if she has to." Sam agreed—until bedtime.

She put the baby in her crib. On cue the baby started screaming. Sam thought she could handle it. Five minutes seemed like five hours. "This is cruel," she decided. "It's even crueler to expect me to suffer through this." She heated a bottle and held the baby, rocking and cooing as the baby drank greedily. When her daughter came home and demanded to know if she had given in, Sam had an impulse to lie. Instead she said, "Yes, and the next time you want me to baby-sit, call when she's toilet trained." If you follow your heart in some matters, be prepared for some potentially angry consequences!

New Ideas Don't Negate Old Values

Singer Gladys Knight has two grandchildren and says that as a grandparent she has some of the same feelings her grandmother had, in that she doesn't agree with everything her children do as parents. For example, when she hears parents complain that *their* parents are spoiling their children, she counters with, "I'd rather risk stepping on the toes of my son and daughter-in-law by picking up a grandchild than listen to a crying spell."

Like many grandparents, she has a contemporary outlook yet a down-home sense of family. She points out, "Lifestyle changes within the black family have created a new breed of grandparents. I'm trying to leave a legacy as an entertainer and entrepreneur so my grandchildren and their children will have the resources to explore their ideas."

The Neatness Issue

When Mimi and Jon's granddaughter, Alex, was three years old she came to visit her grandparents. When she was through playing with her toys, they were strewn all over the room, and Mimi said, "Don't you think you should put your toys away?" In typical three-year-old fashion, Alex put her hands on her hips and said, "Sometimes I do, and sometimes I don't!" Mimi decided she could have this option in her own house and quickly added "pick up toys" to the short list of rules for Grandma's house.

Only One Rule

Speaking of rules, Joan has only one rule for her grand-daughter at her house, and it's regarding food. "I can't stand it when she says she wants to eat something and I get it ready and then she decides she doesn't want it after all," she says. "Now we have one rule—whatever she chooses to eat she must finish it before asking for something else. It's a tiny rule. I don't have any others, and she always obeys it because she knows it's not negotiable."

▶ Good Things Not to Say or Do: ◀ Rules for Grandparents

One wise and all-knowing grandmother has a long list of things grandparents should never say or do if they want to be cool. Here's the short version:

- Never ask your grandchild's parents why they are doing something a certain way. This implies that you disapprove of whatever they're doing.
- Never ask your grandchild which grandparents he likes best. This puts him on the spot.
- Never ever tell your grandchild a story about when her parents were little and did something that wasn't nice. She will want to hear this one over and over again.
- Never say, "She'll lose some of that weight when she starts to walk," or any other comment about physical appearance.
- Never do or say anything to embarrass your grandchild or his parents.
- Never tell off-color jokes or use profanity in front of your grandchildren, even when their parents aren't around. They will absolutely quote you.

- Never smoke around your grandchildren.
- Never comment when your grandchildren are being reprimanded by their parents.
- Never tell a grandchild he can do it at Grandma's house when his parents are telling him to stop doing something.
- Never drop in at your grandchild's house unannounced. Your children won't appreciate this.
- Never make your grandchild's parents feel guilty.
- Never make demands of your children, such as expecting them to come to dinner regularly.

She says she's working on those last two. "It just isn't Sunday if they don't come over. That's grandparent day." Right now she wants her son and daughter-in-law to feel very guilty about not bringing the children to dinner on Sunday for her birthday. "How could they be so inconsiderate as to make other plans for that day?" she laments. "What will you do?" I ask her. "I'm doing it," she says. "I'm calling all my friends and complaining so I'll be over the hurt and anger. Then I'll forget about it."

Her new solution is to ask if she can have the children by themselves so their parents can have a day off. "But, Mom, that's family day," her daughter reminds her. "I'm trying to say nothing, as loud as I can," she says.

The Pacifier Issue

Marjory says, "If you want to see your grandchildren again, learn never to make the mistake I made." When Carly, age three, was still walking around with the pacifier in her mouth, her grandmother said, "When is she going to get over that disgusting habit?" She's since learned to be more tactful and never asks why her grandchildren's parents are doing anything a certain way. "Most of all, I try never to compare the way they do things to the way we used to do them."

The Haircut Issue

When Sara was little she loved to sit on the bathroom counter and let me trim her hair. We played barber, and she held the mirror while I draped a big towel around her shoulders. One day I didn't do such a terrific job and her mother was extremely angry when she saw what I had done. She made me promise never ever to cut her daughter's hair again.

A few months later, while Sara's mother was at the beauty salon getting her own hair cut, Sara begged, "Please, Nana, cut my hair." I told her, "Your mommy doesn't like the way I cut it." "But, Nana, *I* like the way you cut my hair," she reasoned, "and you're her mommy, so she has to do what you tell her." I admit, it was a good argument from a five-year-old, but not good enough.

When my daughter came home, she complained that she hated her new haircut and would never go back there again. Sara looked up and said, "See! You should have let Nana cut it." At times like this it's almost impossible not to gloat, but try.

First-Time Achievements

While Jean was baby-sitting for her one-year-old grandchild, the baby pulled herself up to the edge of the coffee table. Jean sat across the room and, with her arms outstretched, tried to encourage the baby to walk to her. Gingerly the child let go and took two steps before plunking down. When the baby's mother returned, Jean debated about telling her this news. "I decided not to," she said. "I remember the look on her face the first time the baby rolled over. She was so excited, telling me over and over how happy she was to be the first to see this and not the baby-sitter." Jean says, "At that moment I decided if I'm the first to hear her first word, see her first wave, or witness the first clapping hands, I will not report this. I'd rather wait for her parents to tell me about her first achievements, after she does it a second time."

The Grandparent as Substitute Mother

Joan's grandchild lived with her while the child's parents were going through a divorce and relocating to different cities. "It was a very traumatic time for all of us, and it lasted a lot longer than I had anticipated, agreed to, or wanted. But I love Betsy, and she and I had a wonderful six months getting to know each other." The problem was that when Betsy's mother finally sent for her, the child didn't want to leave. She had started kindergarten and was attached to Joan, even on occasion calling her Mama.

"A grandparent should never try to take the place of a child's mother," Joan said. "I had to work hard to come up with all sorts of positive things for the child to look forward to even when I wasn't sure of the outcome."

A year later when her son brought Betsy for a visit, things were a bit strained, but Joan knew she had to accept the situation. "I was grateful that I was able give her loving care during the time we had together. Never once did I say a bad word about her mother. I tried hard to reinforce good feelings about her even though she was giving my son a very hard time. I call Betsy every week, and while her mother never quite warms up to me, she is cordial and never denies me access to my grandchild. It's important for me to keep contact. When she's older maybe she'll call me on her own. At least she knows I care."

What a Cute Little Girl

At eighteen months Cody has long blond curls. He's a chunky baby and to us he's all boy. But even when he's dressed in blue from head to toe, people stop my daughter to exclaim, "What a cute little girl you have!"

That first haircut is always traumatic for the mother. We have learned never to suggest cutting a child's hair. Mothers of little boys do everything possible to avoid cutting off those baby curls. It marks a passage from their infant stage and is hard to give up. My friend Harriet gives the same advice if you have a teenage grandson. "If you want to be cool never suggest that he needs a haircut."

A Temper Tantrum Isn't Cause for Alarm

Zelda has learned to remain calm and not get upset when her grandson throws a fit at the checkout counter. "I know he's just having a bad moment and his behavior in no way reflects on me." Then she apologizes to the people around her, picks him up, and whisks him out of the store, without the candy bar he wanted so badly. "Foolishly, I used to try to reason with him until my daughter said, 'Mom, get real. You can't reason with a two-year-old.' Now when I take him out, I do two things: avoid the candy aisle and bring something in my purse to distract him."

You Have to Run to Keep Up

Jacob remembers the predicament he found himself in after taking his seven-year-old grandson, Bobby, to the movies. "We were walking home," he says, "when he suddenly let go of my hand and decided to tease me by running ahead. I tried to keep up with him, but the closer we got to home the farther away he got. By the time we got home I was way behind him, even though I was making every effort to keep up. When he walked into the house ahead of me, his mother was horrified." "Where's Grandpa?" she asked. "Oh, I left him in the dust," was the child's reply. Jacob says, "All I could do was accept my fate and promise to do better the next time, if there is a next time. I decided to let his mother deal with disciplining him on this one."

7

Special Events, Holidays, and Family Celebrations

Most grandparents use any excuse to visit their grandchildren. Even if we don't have the opportunity to see them often, most families make an effort to get together for the holidays. These family celebrations reinforce our grandchildren's awareness that they are growing up as part of an extended family. The more we share special times together, the more important our sense of family becomes.

 ## Special Events

Special events mark passages in our grandchildren's lives. These include birthdays, a musical recital, a Christmas pageant, or a school event. Grandparents who live near their grandchildren feel lucky to be part of their activities. Those living far away regret missing these events. However, we can participate even when we can't be there in person.

Sharing Birthdays Near and Far

Three of our six grandchildren have summer birthdays. This is the time we see all the children together, and we have festive birthday parties on the deck. All the grandchildren get presents, so even the children we don't see on their birthdays don't feel left out. However, when those children have their birthdays, we always call in the evening, after the party is over, so we can hear all about it from the birthday child. I also try to send a present earlier than the birthday date so my present doesn't get lost among the other gifts. I ask my daughters to let them open it early. This way Grandma's gift is extraspecial!

A Family Birthday Party

Maddy has given elaborate family birthday parties for her six granddaughters since they were born. "I don't care how they celebrate with their friends, I still have everyone to my house over the weekend. I bake a cake with a theme, and we make a big deal out of the birthday girl. I intend to do this for my great-grandchildren as well."

Every Month Is Cause for Celebration

Did you know there is something to celebrate every month? Just look at your calendar and you'll see beyond the obvious holidays to Flag Day, Secretaries' Day, Valentine's Day, Presidents' Days, St. Patrick's Day, Mother's Day, Father's Day, Grandparents' Day, and all sorts of obscure events in your area. Use them as themes for sending cards to your grandchildren. I once sent a "You are the best secretary" card to Tori who likes to help me in my "workroom," as she calls my office. And to Sara, my occasional store helper, I sent a card to celebrate "Employee of the Month." Card stores provide a variety of blank cards. Use these or create your own design on the computer to send a special-occasion greeting to your grandchildren.

Photographing Special Events

Many grandparents who see their grandchildren only on holidays make sure they take lots of pictures or videotape the occasion. We like to make little albums to record these experiences. Sometimes we use them as birthday presents to send to our grandchildren's parents. As a professional photographer, my husband, Jon, thinks people don't edit enough. "They fill their albums with too many pictures, good and bad, rather than just the very best ones." He suggests buying small albums to hold a limited number of photographs. In this way you're forced to be selective, and the overall presentation is more dramatic.

Sharing Memories of a Special Event

Frank and Tonya took their grandchildren to Disney World and took lots of pictures. They then made a wonderful album for the children's parents. The children were able to relive the experience while showing their parents what it looked like and their parents got to see what the children had done with Grandma and Grandpa.

The Recital

It's natural to want to take pictures of your grandchild's first ballet recital, school play, or holiday celebration. However, here's a bit of advice from my in-residence photographer, "If you look at the audience of parents and grandparents attending a child's performance, all you see is a sea of cameras. The event is being recorded, but the family isn't experiencing the event as it's happening. It's just different." He suggests taking a few pictures, then putting the camera down and really focusing your attention on the action. It will be a lot more satisfying and you'll still have the pictures to relive the event.

Grandma of the Bride

When Ruthie's granddaughter was planning a wedding, Ruthie wanted to participate in the ritual shopping experience of a lifetime, buying the wedding gown. "I think she tried on every dress that was ever made," she said. "I didn't realize how difficult it could be to find the perfect dress for the most important event of your life."

Since Ruthie lives in New Jersey and her family lives in Rhode Island, she planned a visit around a weekend that would be devoted to shopping. "Did she find a dress?" I asked. "Not that weekend," Ruthie said. "But I loved being part of this, and when she walked down the aisle I knew she had chosen the most beautiful dress on earth!" Would she go through it again? She says, "I have four more granddaughters. I certainly hope so."

If you live far from your grandchildren and don't want to miss out on the preparations for special events like this, you might schedule a visit to correspond with their plans. Rather than simply participating in the wedding itself, for example, it might be fun to be involved with the events that lead up to it as well. However, keep in mind that planning a wedding is a stressful time for everyone. Be absolutely sure your granddaughter and her mother want you to come along, and don't offer an opinion unless it's solicited. Your attitude should be, whichever dress she chooses, she will be the most beautiful bride who ever walked down the aisle.

A Special Outing

Having an outing with one grandchild at a time is a special event even on an ordinary day. Many grandparents love an outing with a grandchild away from brothers or sisters. This makes the child feel extraspecial and creates a bond between Grandma or Grandpa and child. Depending on the age of the child, having lunch at a nice restaurant, taking a walk in the park, or going to the zoo or a concert can make a day memorable. Sometimes both grandparents take an older grandchild to an event that isn't appropriate for a younger sibling. When our son-in-law's parents took five-year-old Sara to a show, her dad took her younger sister Julia on a train ride. This gave both children special time without the other.

Silly Things

"Remember when we did silly things at your house?" Rebecca reminded her grandma. "When was that?" asked Grandma. "You know, when I came by myself without Zoe and all day we did silly things." Her grandmother can't remember the exact day, which goes to show it doesn't take much to create a special event for a three-year-old. Just having you all to themselves is enough. When I'm in a silly mood I create a Backward Day for a grandchild. We put our clothes on backward and walk backward. We eat dessert first (for one meal only!) and then our lunch. They draw pictures and sign their names backward and I call them by their backward names all day. When the phone rings I let them answer by saying "Good-bye." Four- to six-year-olds love this.

 ## The New Baby

The announcement that a new baby is on the way is always cause for a family to celebrate. However, from that moment on, the soon-to-be-grandparents must be extrasensitive to all sorts of new situations, real and imagined, that arise. If you thought your children's wedding was fraught with emotional clashes . . . well, let's just say it's a time to tread lightly.

It's a Boy!

When my youngest daughter gave birth to her second son, I stopped at the hospital gift shop before going up to her room and hastily grabbed a balloon from the large container. You can't believe how foolish I felt, when on entering the room my son-in-law exclaimed, "It's a Girl!?" which is what the balloon read. That was about the uncoolest thing I've ever done. Fortunately, Cody's parents have a sense of humor. They even made me pose for a picture holding the baby and the balloon. At least I didn't say, "He looks like a little monkey," or, "He'll get cuter. They all look like little old men when they're born." In other words, choose your words (and your balloons) carefully!

Names Are a Personal Matter

The minute your children announce that a new baby is on the way, the grandparents begin to suggest names. All of my daughters learned a valuable lesson—the second time around. When they were pregnant with their second children, they refused to discuss the names they were considering.

"As soon as you tell your family what names you like," my daughter said, "everyone has an opinion. Either it reminds them of a bully they knew in high school, or there was a distant relative whom everyone detested with that name, or they are insulted because the child will be named after someone on the other side of the family."

Maggie, the grandmother of five, has this advice for soon-to-be-grandparents: "Whatever name the parents choose for their newborn, always tell them you love it, even if you think it's the worst name you've ever heard." She goes on to report from experience, "The moment the child is born, your attitude will change and you will actually come to think the name is perfect. If not, pretend, for your own sake." If you have an opinion, don't offer it unless solicited and, even then, know that this can backfire and the name you suggest will go into the "Not in This Lifetime" file.

The Christening or Briss

An older sibling often feels left out during this important celebration. Always send a small gift for the other children, along with the newborn gift. This is a way of saying, "Congratulations on having a new brother or sister." However, at a family gathering for a christening or briss, many people bring gifts for or pay attention only to the baby. An older child may feel left out. As grandparents, this is a wonderful opportunity to lavish attention on the big brother or big sister and play up the important role he or she now has.

Barbara told her three-year-old grandson, Robby, "Your

new baby brother will learn so many things from you because you're so smart." But then she cautions, "Don't emphasize his responsibility too much. I also like to tell him what fun it will be to have someone to play with all the time."

Big Brother, Big Sister Celebration

When Connie's third child was born, her parents had a party for their extended family. The invitation read, "Come to a Big Sister, Big Brother Celebration." The baby was tucked away in his crib, and the attention was centered on the older children. Everyone congratulated them, not their parents, and there were games like follow the big sister, where the children and their cousins took turns being the leader and the little brothers and sisters had to follow. Or a version of Simon Says called Big Brother Says. Everyone received little gifts.

Later, when the children were having their cake and ice cream, the family oohed and aahed over the new baby, rather than at the very beginning of the party. By this time the other children weren't so aware of the divided attention.

The Best Gift

When Marjory's son and daughter-in-law had their first baby, she went over to help out for a few days. "When I left," she said, "I stocked the freezer with meals to be used later. My daughter-in-law told me this was the best gift I could have given them."

Don't Overstay Your Welcome

Another new grandmother I know who lives in the same town as her children says, "I always wait to be invited over. I stay long enough for my daughter to take a nap or go out to do a few errands, which gives me time alone with the baby, and then I leave. I know if I stay too long I won't be so welcome the next time. And my daughter knows I have to get back to work, so she doesn't take advantage of me by staying out too long."

When a New Brother or Sister Arrives

Recognizing the problems that can occur when a new sibling arrives, grandparents Chris and Harold take care of the new baby as often as possible so his parents can have quality time with their older child. In this way he has his parents all to himself and is reassured that the baby hasn't replaced him.

Lie if You Have To

"We've decided to name the baby Consuela," Vanessa's daughter announced. "That's a lovely name," Vanessa said, even though in her heart of hearts she was hoping they'd name the baby Emily after her father, the child's maternal grandfather, Emil. When she spoke to a friend, Vanessa said, "My only hope is that they'll take one look at that brand-new face and be thunderstruck by how much she resembles my father."

Supreme Tactfulness

When Roland laid eyes on his new granddaughter he was tempted to comment on her beautiful features and tell the new parents how much she resembled his mother. "Seeing my daughter-in-law holding that new baby I suddenly realized she might be offended by this." Instead he said, "She is so beautiful. She seems to have gotten the best features from both of you."

Family Gatherings and Holidays

Whenever three generations come together there's the potential for fireworks. But it's also a time for families to spend meaningful, quality time together and have a lot of fun. Cool grandparents know how to keep the peace, keep everything light and fun, and they never use the time to criticize, reprimand, tell unpleasant stories about when their children were young, or do anything to embarrass the parents of their grandchildren. My mother had a saying, "All the things you do with your children and grandchildren are building memories for their futures." Grandparents have a wonderful opportunity to make memories of family gatherings some of the very best.

Your House or Theirs?

Georgia and Ken remember their first Christmas in their first house when their first baby was born. "We had always gone to Ken's father's house for Christmas, but that year we wanted to have Christmas in our brand-new home. We wanted to enjoy the day through our baby's eyes and watch her having her first Christmas." She says this presented a problem. "We had a difficult time convincing Ken's father to break with tradition by coming to our house. Now, as grandparents, we don't expect our kids to come here for Christmas and usually plan to visit them, if not on the day, at some time between Christmas and New Year's." They suggest, "Try to stay flexible about the holidays, and everyone will have a much better time. Don't take it personally if they spend holidays at their home or at the in-laws'. If you can, try to schedule a visit during the holdiay season and enjoy the time you have." Some grandparents have children and grandchildren scattered around the country. It's almost impossible for everyone to get together every year. Therese and Woody rotate their Christmases by visiting the grandchildren in one part of the country one year and the others the next.

Thanksgiving Weekend

Thanksgiving is particularly hectic at our house because we get together with three sets of parents, each with two children. The weekend usually lasts from Wednesday through Sunday, so it's really closer to a week. It means putting our lives on hold, including our work schedule. Our weekend usually starts with eager anticipation, tapers off to wondering if we'll survive a household of six little children all taking naps at different times or not at all, and ends with the inevitable letdown when they leave. During their visit we try to plan a little time alone with each child, usually away from the house.

If your family is coming to you, you'll probably be doing some cooking during this holiday weekend. Try to involve a grandchild with the easier projects. What might seem like a chore to you, peeling and mashing potatoes, for example, is great fun for a six-year-old. In fact, just being in the kitchen, coloring at the table while you're cooking, can lead to some interesting conversations with a grandchild.

The Best-Laid Plans

For all my good intentions, things don't always work out as planned. This year I decided to set a beautiful Thanksgiving table using all the family heirlooms. I laid out my great-grandmother's lace tablecloth, my mother's ornate silverware and candlesticks, and absolutely no paper napkins, even for children. There would be no children's table even though they are, with only one exception, all under six. I lit candles and placed a bowl filled with little gifts for each child in the center.

When it came time for dinner, the kids just wanted the presents and to sit at the "little table" where they usually have their meals together. I shrugged. Over the years I've learned to be flexible no matter what I've planned ahead of time. Their parents were just as happy. I'll try this again in about ten years.

Putting Things Into Perspective

One Thanksgiving, when the kids were running around and it seemed incredibly chaotic, the daughter living farthest away announced, "This is the last time we're coming for Thanksgiving. It's just too hectic and it's a lot of trouble and the kids don't really get quality time with you anyway." Then Jon reminded her, "Every summer when I was growing up, my parents, aunts and uncles, and cousins rented little cottages next to one another at the Jersey shore. Looking back I don't know how any of the adults could stand it. All they seemed to do was make meals and break up squabbles. But those get-togethers provided me with the best memories of my childhood, and that's what you're providing for your children." They all came for Thanksgiving the following year.

Making Time With Each Child

Often when our family gets together, the kids are busy playing with all their cousins. It's almost impossible to have quality time with each of them. As grandparents it's entertaining to watch them playing and relating to one another, but it isn't the same as relating one-to-one.

Some grandparents see all their grandchildren together to give their parents time alone. Others take each child for a separate outing. Rose and Lewis's daughter drops their two granddaughters off at their house every Sunday. Rose says, "Lewis sometimes reads to Anna while I do a puzzle with Elizabeth." This gives each child a little one-on-one time with each grandparent.

Relaxing Your Standards

Sally used to get excited when the whole family came for holiday meals. "I made elaborate celebrations and enjoyed doing it. However, as I've gotten older, I don't have the energy to do it all myself, but my kids and grandkids still expect it."

When two more grandchildren were added to their already large family, Sally decided to assign chores to each parent as well as the children, in keeping with their ages. "I discovered what fun it can be to let a three-year-old set the table. I had to lower my standards a great deal, but Jody felt so accomplished when everyone praised him for his table-setting skills. I have to admit, it wasn't anything like my table settings, but I learned to accept the way the children had all done their chores. The funny thing is, nobody thought of it as a chore. This holiday was a lot more relaxed."

Table Settings by the Kids

When Sara was in preschool she learned to draw a turkey by placing her hand, with fingers spread, on the paper and drawing around each finger and her palm. The thumb was the turkey's head and she added little stick legs. One Thanksgiving I suggested that she make a place card for every member of the family. She colored each one and together we wrote each person's name on them. She put one on each plate.

Tori likes to decorate, so she was given the job of using my assortment of tiny pumpkins, gourds, pinecones, nuts, and Indian corn to make an arrangement on the table. Then she went around the house gathering all my little framed photographs and placed them here and there on the table as well. For another Thanksgiving the kids used black markers to write names on gourds and small pumpkins to use as place cards.

You can tailor this activity to the specific holiday. When the little children do something creative like this, I never change a thing. When everyone comes to the table we all express enthusiasm over their contributions.

Chalkboard Fun

One summer when the kids were coming to visit, Jon devised a unique play table for the kids that turned out to be the center of all their activities during the entire summer.

The top of the table was made from a piece of slate such as they use for blackboards (purchased from a local home center), which we supported on concrete building blocks. These are sturdy and you can make the table height exactly right for small children. Upside-down milk crates will work as well. We then placed railroad ties (from a lumberyard) on each side to be used as their seats. I bought big, fat sidewalk chalk and divided it into four plastic pails. Blackboard erasers, sponges, or rags can be used for wiping the slate clean. The table was used for outdoor dining whenever the children visited and it provided endless fun.

Easter Egg Hunt

Our grandchildren often visit over Easter weekend. We like to take them to the local Easter egg hunt held on the grounds of the hospital. The smallest children don't always find as many eggs as the older ones. In fact, sometimes they don't find any, and this causes tears, temper tantrums, or just sadness. The first year that happened to Tori it almost broke my heart. Now I make sure to tuck a few candy eggs in my pocket, then place them strategically for the little ones to find.

 Vacations

I knew a man who had worked very hard all his life. By middle age he was financially well off. His story isn't so different from that of other men his age. "I never had time to enjoy my children when they were growing up. Now I have grandchildren, and I'm enjoying them in a way I never could with my own children. I feel so lucky to have grandchildren." Once a year this grandfather plans an all-expense-paid vacation with his children and their children.

This idea is one of my most often expressed fantasies, for when I win the lottery.

I talked to many grandparents who regularly plan wonderful vacations with their extended families, and it sounds pretty terrific. I received all sorts of interesting ideas and good advice, many that don't involve spending a lot of money. Some grandparents take their grandkids camping, some go to family camps through church organizations, some go on fishing trips. There are many resources for traveling with grandchildren. You'll find the names and numbers at the end of this chapter.

A Family Affair

Marion is the director of a community preschool. She and her husband own a restaurant in the town where they live. Her children are also involved with the restaurant. She has thirteen grandchildren. Every year the entire family plans a vacation together. One year they rented a huge house at the seashore. Another time they went to a resort. She says, "Everyone looks forward to these vacations. Best of all, Joe and I are on vacation too. It's a whole different experience from relating to your kids and grandkids at your house or theirs. You're all on neutral ground. Our children don't have to be constantly parenting, because everyone is sharing in the responsibility for everyone else. It's a little like being on a kibbutz. We absolutely love it and it reinforces our relationships."

All Together at the Seashore

I see many extended families vacationing at the beach in the summertime. This is a great way for everyone to relate to one another in a most relaxing way. It makes me realize that just providing a wonderful setting is enough. The children and parents don't have to be on the go all day long, which makes everyone grouchy and tired at the end of the day.

When my children go to see my mother in Florida, she thinks she should plan things for them to do. "Let's just hang out at the beach," they tell her. Many grandparents living in the South get so used to having the warm weather and beach they forget what a natural resource they have to offer their visiting grandchildren. No other activities can compete. Safety Note: Our favorite pediatrician, Dr. Mike, says: "If you're in charge of your grandchildren at the beach, don't take your eyes off them for a second and always slather them from head to toe with number 30 sunscreen."

Away at Home

We live in a vacation spot, so our kids and grandkids come here on their vacation. We have to plan our work schedules in order to have vacation time together.

To make it a bit more like a vacation for us when they come, we plan special outings. On hot evenings everyone prepares different parts of a picnic dinner and we take everything down to the beach around five o'clock. The crowds have gone home, the kids run around, we watch the sun go down. When we go home, there's nothing to clean up, the kids go to bed, and it's as if we've all been on vacation. Best of all, neither grandparent has to cook meals after working all day.

If you don't live in a vacation place, have an at-home vacation in your backyard. Set up a tent and let the kids have a sleepover. Roast marshmallows on the grill and do all sorts of things you'd do on vacation. Have one rule: Nobody goes in the house, except to use the bathroom. The idea is to pretend you're away.

Fun for All

Joanna and Dan went away with their daughter, son-in-law, and their four children under five years old for the Christmas holiday. "It was wonderful," Joanna said. "We went to Colorado to a ski lodge. The kids had fun playing in the snow and we took them sledding and did all sorts of outdoor activities. Their parents skied a little." Choose a place where there is enough to entertain families of all ages, and your vacation will be a success.

Do Your Research

Bill and Ann like to vacation with their grandchildren alone without their parents. This also gives their children a vacation. "It's important to remember that you're responsible for their safety, but you also want to have fun," Ann says. "One year we took them to New York City. We researched all the age-appropriate things that were advertised in *The New York Times.* We checked out the Internet and wrote to the convention and visitors bureau (available in any city you want to visit). We sent away for tickets in advance where needed and planned meals and transportation accordingly. For example, some places were within walking distance of the hotel. Others were easily accessible by bus or subway. For evening activities we allocated funds for taxi rides, and we allowed enough time between activities for walking and sightseeing.

"Taking three teenagers to a large city is tricky. You have to know your way around, the best way to get to each place, and how to pace yourself." Bill says that the most important thing is to have each day planned out and then allow for flexibility if something interesting presents itself. He also suggests carrying a map of the area you're visiting at all times. Find out if you can get discount passes for things like transportation, museums, and sights. Some tour groups provide guided tours to major cities. (See page 131 for travel resources.)

Going to a Hotel

Jon and I were once invited to a wedding in a town close to where our children live. The reception was held in a large hotel where we would be staying. We decided to use the wedding as an excuse to plan a family vacation and rented connecting rooms for our children and grandchildren. It was a cold winter weekend. Everyone brought bathing suits and workout clothes. It was an evening wedding, so we played all day.

While we were at the wedding, the parents with babies ordered room service and watched TV while those with older kids ate in one of the hotel dining rooms. During the day we all went swimming together in the indoor pool and relaxed in the whirlpool. The kids played video games. It was a great weekend and one you can re-create easily, even if you don't have a wedding to attend.

Room Service Was Invented by a Grandparent

Helen can't afford a real vacation with her teenage granddaughter, but now and then they spend a night together in a local hotel. They order a great dinner from room service, choose a movie to watch, then snuggle up and talk half the night away. They sleep late in the morning and go home feeling like they've been away for a long time. "We've been doing this since she was ten, and I hope we'll continue forever," Helen says. She suggests finding out about different hotel chains and what they offer. Some have exercise and game rooms, pools, and full-service health spas.

Vacationing With Great-Grandparents

Every summer my daughters invite my mother to spend part of their vacation time with them and their families. In this way my mother gets to see her grandchildren as parents and her great-grandchildren growing up, even though she lives in Florida and they live in the Northeast. One day Sara said, "I like being with Grandma Ruth because she never says, 'Hurry up, Sara.' "

I tried to explain that her mommy wants her to get to school or her swim lesson on time and sometimes she dawdles. "I know," she said, "but Grandma Ruth is old and she doesn't have anyplace to go, so I like that better." My mother, who has a very active life, doesn't think of herself as old with no place to go, but says she's happy to comply by slowing down to the pace of a six-year-old if it means getting the award for Most Popular Great-Grandma.

Hearing this comment from Sara reminds me that children live in a timeless world. Adults are on a defined time schedule. If we, as grandparents, can suspend time and let go of external pressures when we're with our grandchildren, we can experience the magic of the child's world.

Sharing Interests

Jerry and Selma live in a retirement community on a golf course in North Carolina. Whenever their children and grandchildren used to visit, they complained that they never saw Grandpa Jerry. He was always on the golf course. He decided to solve the problem by getting his daughter and son-in-law interested in the game. When his first grandchild was old enough he bought her a set of small clubs and began to teach her how to play. "One day there will be three generations on the golf course," he says. "It will be a lot of fun when they come down and we can all play together."

A Week Without Parents

Henrietta and Carl offered to baby-sit for their three schoolage grandchildren during their spring break. "Why don't we make it a real vacation for all of us?" Carl suggested. The children lived in a city, so Grandma and Grandpa thought it would be fun for them to experience a rural environment. They packed the car and took off to a cabin they had rented near a lake. They brought fishing and hiking gear, and it turned out to be an enriching week for everyone. Without parents, the children and grandparents could relate more openly and get to know each other better.

More and more grandparents are traveling alone with their grandchildren. Travel tours are expanding their services to include guided tours of major cities, packaged weeklong stays at a dude ranch, tours through the Rockies by rail, or white-water rafting. The Sierra Club offers an annual outing called "Just for Grandparents and Grandchildren" based at a lodge in the Sierra Nevadas in California. (See below for information.)

Resources for Traveling With Grandchildren

When planning a trip with your grandchildren, start with a short trip. Be sure children are ready to spend time away from their parents and won't get homesick in the middle of the trip. Having them stay overnight at your house first may give you a chance to evaluate their readiness. The following trip organizers will send you information about different kinds of trips for different age groups:

AFC Tours: 619-481-8188
American Wilderness Experience: 1-800-444-3833
Club Med: 1-800-258-2633
Franklyn D. Resort: 1-800-654-1337
Grandtravel: 1-800-247-7651
Maupintours: 1-800-255-6162
Premier Cruise Lines (The Big Red Boat):
    1-800-373-2654
Sierra Club: 415-977-5522
Visatours: 1-800-248-4782

8

Activities

Before visiting our grandchildren, Jon and I take a walk on the beach and gather a bag full of shells. In the fall and winter especially, we find large clamshells that don't seem to wash up in the summertime. We take these along with little bottles of poster paints and brushes, and one of the projects we do with the kids is painting shells. Before our last visit, the beach was covered with snow and we weren't able to collect the shells. When we arrived, the little girls said, "Nana and Pop Pop, you forgot to bring shells." I didn't realize what a ritual this had become.

Depending on your interests, there are all sorts of activities to do with grandchildren of all ages. Even helping to make a bed can be fun for a three-year-old. When Kaitlin visited her grandmother, the four-year-old said, "Grammy,

what special thing can we do?" Her grandmother was in the middle of spring cleaning and said, "How about, let's wash the kitchen floor!" "Yeah!" exclaimed Kaitlin as she merrily got out the mop and pail.

 ## Simple Pleasures

Kids are happy doing almost anything with their grandparents because they get their grandparents' undivided attention. The simplest projects, games, and activities create lasting memories. When I asked several kids of different ages what they liked most about their grandparents, the unanimous reply was, "They always have time for me."

Chores That Are Fun

Children love to sharpen pencils, and an electric pencil sharpener is a harmless and, I've discovered, indestructible tool. Once you teach a grandchild how to sharpen pencils, it is his job for life. The trick is never ever to sharpen a

 pencil yourself, because the goal is to have plenty of dull pencils in waiting at all

times. When your grandchild shows up you simply exclaim, "I'm so glad you came. All my pencils need sharpening and I haven't had the time to get to them." This keeps the child distracted for at least twenty minutes! Remember to tell him: Pencils get sharpened on only one end.

Building

When we were having some work done on our house, our grandson was fascinated with the builders and wanted to help. We set him up with a workbench, scraps of wood he collected with his grandfather at the dump (another great activity), and basic tools. Keep in mind, a building project isn't a chance to give a shop lesson. Hammering nails into boards is fun, and having no particular agenda gives the child a chance to be creative, if only in his imagination.

Their Own Spaces

A grandparent's home isn't complete without a grandchild shelf, drawer, and a small table or desk appropriately stocked with his or her office supplies. This should include the following: lots of lined and unlined paper, a package of construction paper, lots of colored and regular pencils, erasers, glue, sequins, stickers, safety scissors, paper clips, coloring books, crayons, and water-soluble markers.

Fill a plastic milk crate with age-appropriate craft and office supplies and let the child know these are his private office supplies. I once found an old-fashioned school desk with a lift-up top and an attached seat at a yard sale. The desk, a permanent fixture in my office, is in constant use and I replenish its supplies often. Between visits, I remove scribbled pages from the coloring books so they always seem new. The desk is perfect for two- to six-year-olds, and when they visit, they do their "work" in Nana's office, right next to me.

Yard Sale Toys

Every time I go to a yard sale or the Salvation Army I look for toys and books in good condition. I buy things for all ages because the interests and ages of my grandchildren change with every visit. They always go right to the bottom cabinet in my office to see what new things await them. From time to time my daughters weed out the toys the children have outgrown, and we donate them to our hospital thrift shop. In our town, recycling is an ongoing community effort. Note: Used plastic toys should be sterilized in boiling water before being given to young children.

Keep It Short and Sweet

Whatever you plan to do with your grandchild, keep it short, keep it simple, and don't be discouraged if it doesn't turn out to be perfect. You won't have to worry that you've overdone a good thing. Your grandchild will let you know when it's time to end the activity.

Playing Dress Up

Gertrude's grandchildren love to play dress up. "When they come I let them put on makeup, dress up in all my clothes, and wear anything they want no matter how outrageous." She says no toys she could buy them would provide as much fun and keep them busy for so long. If you don't want the kids to wear your clothing, you can find cheap, wonderful dress-up items at your local thrift shop or at garage sales. Think frilly and lacy or funky and offbeat. The kids will love those tie-dyed shirts from the sixties. They're back in style! Great items to look for include hats, gloves, petticoats (remember crinolines?), scarves, costume jewelry, high-heeled shoes, cowboy boots, anything made from shiny or soft fabric.

A Plain Old Box

The best toys aren't really toys at all but the things that fuel a child's imagination. The most ordinary items around the house, actually castoffs, can provide the longest and most amusing playtime.

A discarded cardboard box that once contained a new television set has become the most coveted plaything in our house. Every grandchild has used this as a house, a store, a tent, a spaceship, a train, a hideout, and any number of other imaginative dwellings. They have colored and decorated it and turned the flaps into doors. From time to time one of us will walk by and knock on the roof. "Anybody home?" I'll inquire. "No," a little voice will answer. It's a wonderful place for a child to get some private time away from siblings.

Grandma's Spa

When Marilyn has her granddaughters, Emma and Hannah, to stay at her house, she treats them to a day at her "spa." "This is a great way to spend a rainy or wintry cold afternoon," she suggests. "We make a big ritual out of running the bubble bath. We arrange all the creams and lotions to spread on our bodies. They each pick out a nail polish color and we do fingers and toes. I let them put on makeup made with natural ingredients that won't harm their skin, and they love it when I have them lie down and put slices of cucumbers on their eyelids. They think this is terribly silly. Then we do exercises to my Jane Fonda tape, after which we have a healthful yogurt and vegetable lunch with fresh fruit.''

Bubble Fun

All little children love blowing bubbles. Claire always brings a bottle of bubble liquid for each of her grandchildren. She advises giving each child his or her own bottle to avoid fights over the one wand inside. "It's messy," she says. "However, the good thing is, it's only soapy water, so even though their fingers and clothes get wet it's harmless."

"This is a great way to teach the little ones hand-eye coordination," says my child-development expert, Grandma Rose. "They learn to dip the wand into the liquid and then to aim and blow through the eye of the wand to produce a stream of bubbles. The more they do this the better they get at it."

"It's great outdoor fun for minimal expense," Claire says. "I always put a bottle of bubble stuff in my purse when we go off to the playground. It's a perfect distraction when one of the children falls or gets into the inevitable tussle over a toy in the sandbox."

Nature Walks

Tess knows the names of all living things, at least according to her grandchildren. "We always walk in the woods, and I describe the things we're looking at. We take little plastic bags and collect pinecones, leaves, twigs, flowers, and even bugs. Sometimes we pretend to be on a safari and call out the names of pretend animals we see hiding behind trees or off in a distance."

At home Tess has the children make a scrapbook of the things they've collected. "I've taught them how to press flowers, which they love. We put the fresh buds they pick between pieces of paper towel and weight them down with several books. After a few days the flowers are dried and pressed, and we place them on the page in the scrapbook. Then we protect them with a sheet of clear plastic Contact paper. We mark the name of the flower and the date, and sometimes the children have me write a little note about our day together." She says this might be, "Today we saw a bunny run across the path." Or, "A ladybug landed on Kathy's finger."

Each time the children visit they love to look back over their mementos from previous excursions. For Christmas this year, Tess gave them a real flower press made of wood, with special papers for preserving the flowers.

Pond Creatures

If you live near a pond, you can introduce your grandchildren to a whole world of living creatures. Take a gallon jar with you on your walk and fill it halfway with pond water (just scoop it right out of the pond). Make holes in the top of the lid and leave it for a few days. Check it from 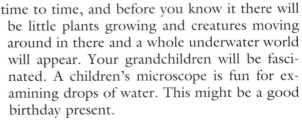 time to time, and before you know it there will be little plants growing and creatures moving around in there and a whole underwater world will appear. Your grandchildren will be fascinated. A children's microscope is fun for examining drops of water. This might be a good birthday present.

A Toddler's Pleasure

You don't have to knock yourself out keeping a toddler busy. Nothing delights her more than the game of heaping gifts on Grandpa. She will pile books, magazines, pillows, toys, and other objects within reach into your lap for as long as you allow this game to go on. Then all you need do is say, "Now take all these things and put them on the table." This can go on, back and forth, for as long as you can stand it. She will never tire of it before you do.

To make it more educational, simply say, "Bring Grandpa the book," to which she may respond with something else, and you can say, "No, that's the candlestick. Now find the book," until she gets it right. Then say, "Very good." This is how grandparents develop the reputation for having patience.

Make Believe

When Tori, age four, comes to play at LaLa's house she always says, "Can I do my store?" She's created a whole world in my walk-in closet. She turns on the light, brings in my little dressing table stool, and sets up her wares that include my bedside clock, a few framed photographs, books, and any other small items she can find around my bedroom. Then she calls out, "LaLa, the store is open." That's my cue to become the customer. I pick up and ask the price of each item, buy it with pretend money, and thank her for being so helpful. I leave the store only to return everything immediately so she can sell them to me all over again.

If I'm busy when she comes to visit, she brings the dolls into the closet to act as customers. But this is not nearly as satisfying and she often forgoes the game until I can take a break. When another grandchild is around they take turns being the customer and the salesperson.

Problem Solving

Andrew, age ten, often comes up with imaginative solutions that are usually a result of a problem he's had that needs solving. Lately, however, he's called to complain about one nuisance or another that he's encountered. For example, the other day he went to the video store to rent the latest Nintendo game player and two video games, only to find they didn't have any players available. He called Grandpa to say, "It makes me so mad. The store has only two machines and once a kid rents one, he keeps it for a whole week, because the store lets you have it for free on the weekend if you get it during the week."

This was very frustrating to him. His entrepreneurial grandfather suggested, hypothetically, that they go into the business of buying the machines and renting them out. "How many do you think we'd need to service all the kids who would want it at one time?" he asked. Then together they figured out what the machines would cost and how much they could rent them for and what they would pay for the video games and how long it would take to get a return on their money. This was purely an exercise, as tomorrow Andrew will be into solving another problem in his life. But for now they could have a little fun and a stimulating "business" conversation. And, of course, Grandpa had the security of knowing he wasn't actually going to be called on to do it. You might try to have a conversation like this, inventing a fictional problem to encourage a grandchild to think logically and get excited about something of interest.

The Lemonade Stand

Selling lemonade is as popular today with children as it was when we were kids. Since this activity involves spending money before the children make money, it's a good way to teach them the basics of commerce, depending on their ages.

Take them to the store to buy the lemonade mix or ingredients. Tell them that you will advance them the money to buy supplies, but make them keep track of the expenses and let them know how the process works: They must first pay you back before they make a profit. They'll also need small paper cups and lots of ice.

Set up the table as suggested for selling seashells on page 143. If you want to get into this, you might work with the children to determine how much they should charge for each cup of lemonade, based on what it cost to make, how many they need to sell to break even, and how much money they can make if they sell all the lemonade for which they have ingredients.

Children under ten years old probably won't be interested in the finances of selling, just the activity. They might want to make cookies to go along with their lemonade. One enterprising group of children who set up a stand each summer on our street give away a cookie with every fifty-cent cup of lemonade. On one particularly hot afternoon they set up their stand in front of a building site. The work crew kept them in business all afternoon, keeping Grandpa in the kitchen turning out pitcher after pitcher because the little entrepreneurs were too busy to leave their stand untended.

Easy Craft Projects

No matter the ages of your grandchildren, craft projects are always fun to do together. Even if you think you're all thumbs, there are lots of quick and easy projects that don't require skill or a particularly creative bent. I've found that having paintbrushes, a drawing pad, and little pots of water-soluble paint are enough to excite any child's imagination.

Painting Shells

This is a good activity for summertime. A walk on the beach is the beginning of this activity. We take a plastic bag for each child and make a game of how many different types of shells we can find. If you don't have access to a beach, most craft stores sell bags of shells. Or you can dig for small stones and rocks in the garden. Once home, we soak the shells in hot, soapy water. Rinse and place them out on a dishtowel to dry.

Next, we cover an outdoor table with newspaper and put out little plastic or paper cups of water, several inexpensive paintbrushes, and jars of poster paints in different colors. For very young children you might pour a little bit of each color paint into sections of an ice cube tray. The materials are all sold in craft and hobby stores, home centers, and five-and-dimes. Most children will jump right in and begin painting. But if a child doesn't know how to begin, suggest making a rainbow of different colors or covering a shell with polka dots. This is easy and will get him or her started. Show them how to rinse the brushes in the cups of water between colors. Your job is to keep emptying and refilling the water cups.

When the children tire of this activity, leave the shells to dry while they go inside for a snack. When they return, the shells will be ready to display. Let them arrange them around the house on shelves, tables, wherever they want. Wrap a particularly beautiful creation in tissue, add a ribbon, and suggest they present it as a gift to their parents or a favorite teacher.

The Seashell Stand

If your grandchildren are particularly enterprising they might want to sell their shells. This involves setting up a table, much as you would for selling lemonade. You'll need a sign that says "Shells for Sale" made from poster board or shirt cardboard. Help the child make this in his or her handwriting. Tack it to the table, a fence on the property, or a nearby tree. Have the children make little price signs from folded pieces of cardboard, much like place cards, so they will stand up next to the shells.

When our grandson, Andrew, was five, he and the next-door neighbor's four-year-old set up their selling table, complete with chairs, at the end of our driveway. They made up the prices for each shell based on size and how much they liked their artwork. They decided the shells should be five, six, and seven cents. Trying to convince them to make the prices a nickel, a dime, and a quarter was useless, so I backed away from my logical suggestions and simply provided them with a box filled with pennies I knew they would need to make change. The problem was, they didn't know how to make change.

As it turned out, most people simply gave them more money, which made them feel they hadn't gotten enough. To them, two coins of any denomination were more than one. But it's still better to let them make the rules.

If you don't live where people pass by, take the kids to

a park or some other public place to set up their temporary "store" and let them get a feel for selling their artwork. They'll love it. Don't forget to go for a treat, which they buy with their profits, right after the sale is over. This gives them a feeling of cause and effect.

Simple Indoor Crafts

The little girls in our family have dolls and a variety of clothing for them. Craft shops sell all sorts of items like straw hats that fit any size doll, sequins, beads, ribbon roses, and other trims. Decorating a hat is easy and fun for a child of three or older. Buy enough material to make a variety to choose from as well as small bottles of Elmer's glue (one for each child). Don't buy beads and such that are too tiny for small children to work with and look good to eat.

Since the sequins and beads usually come in little packages or containers that tip over and spill the contents everywhere, put them into separate bowls or sections of ice cube trays for easy handling. Cover the table with newspaper.

Give each child a hat and a glue bottle and, if you have one hat for yourself, you can show them how to get started. That's all they need. Some children will be satisfied with one item on the hat, others will cover it completely. When they've finished they can have a doll fashion show.

Tie-Dye Flowers

This is a great project for children between four and twelve years of age. You probably have all the materials needed right in your home, so this can be a spur-of-the-moment project when you need one. Since water is involved, it can be a little messy and best done outdoors. But it's not bad for a kitchen tabletop if you cover the table with newspaper.

Materials
    package of cone-shaped coffee filters
    food coloring
    3 or 4 bowls of warm water
    rubber bands
    newspaper
    package of pipe cleaners or wire stems (from a garden
      supply center)
    tongs

Directions

1. Spread the newspaper on a work surface. Add a few drops of food coloring to each bowl of water.
2. Fold a coffee filter lengthwise two or three times and wrap with rubber bands.
3. Hold the filter with tongs and dip it into one of the bowls of colored water.
4. Keep dipping until it is saturated with colored water.
5. Put the cone on the newspaper. Repeat with another cone in another color until you have three or four different-colored cones.
6. Let the filters dry for a few minutes and then remove the rubber bands.
7. Spread the filters out flat and let dry completely. You can use a hair dryer to speed the process.
8. Place the dried filters on top of each other and insert a pipe cleaner or wire stem up through the center about a half inch. Twist the bottom of the filters around the stem and secure with a rubber band. Then turn the filter petals down and arrange in a vase or stick into florist's foam set into a container.

If you want to get fancy you can cut the edges of the filter with pinking shears or cut a scalloped edge all around.

Crayon Rubbings

Because we live in a historic town, there are graveyards with gravestones dating back more than two hundred years. Some of them are inscribed with interesting sayings or designs. Gravestone rubbings can be a fascinating project for children, but you can also do rubbings on a tree trunk, leaf, rock, or anything else with texture. To make a rubbing you need plain paper and crayons. We buy oversize, fat black crayons sold specifically for this purpose in art stores. Place the paper over the textured surface and rub the crayon across the paper a few times. The design will appear. If you take along a roll of masking tape, it will help hold the paper in position, especially when placed against a gravestone.

Decorative Crayon Box

A metal Band-Aid box is perfect for holding crayons and is an easy item for a child to paint and decorate.

Materials
　　large-size box
　　one color of poster or acrylic paint
　　paintbrush
　　small scissors
　　craft glue
　　a pretty picture such as a flower or an animal found on
　　　　wrapping paper, a greeting card, or in a magazine
　　clear nail polish (optional)

Directions

1. Paint the box and let it dry. The paint will dry quickly. Rinse the brush in water.
2. Cut out a flower or other item from the paper.
3. Spread glue on the back of the design and press it onto the front of the painted box. You can add designs around the sides and back if desired. Wipe away any glue that oozes out from the edges of the picture with a damp sponge. Let dry.
4. Coat the front of the box, right over the cutout design, with clear nail polish to protect it and make the surface shiny.

Shell Necklace

At six years of age Samantha loves to make jewelry. Her favorite project is a necklace made of shells. She says, "The inside of the shells is so smooth and I like to find shells that are the same size and paste a little design inside. Sometimes I decorate them with stickers. For Valentine's Day I made a necklace with hearts for my Grandma. This is how I do it." Note: Look for shells with a hole in the top. You will find that enough shells have holes so you can discard those that don't.

Materials
    about 7 small shells
    6 small beads (from five-and-dime, craft, or sewing store)
    magazine to cut out designs, or stickers
    glue
    20-inch-long elastic string (also from the sewing store)

Note: If you don't have shells, use large beads instead.

Directions

1. Put a different sticker inside each shell. Or cut out designs from a magazine that will fit inside the shells and glue one inside each shell. "This is an easy way to glue the little design inside the shell," Samantha says. "Squirt a little bit of glue on some newspaper. Then dip a Q-tip in the glue and paint a spot of the glue on the inside of the shell. Put your cutout on the glue in the shell and press down."

2. Put one end of the elastic string through the tiny hole of one shell. Center the shell on the string and tie a knot to hold it in place.

3. Place a small bead on one end of the string and slide it down right next to the shell.

4. Alternate shells and beads. Always make a knot after you string a shell but not the beads. Your necklace will have three shells and three beads on each side of the center shell.

5. Tie the two ends of the string together and slip the necklace over your head. That's all there is to it.

"If you have a little sister, she can make a necklace with only one shell and a sticker to wear around her neck," Samantha adds.

Starter Plant

When city-born Rebecca came to visit her grandma in the suburbs, Grandma Phyllis asked, "Have you ever planted seeds?" The child had never done this. "We're going to decorate your very own planter and put dirt and seeds in it. When you go home you can put it on your windowsill and soon you'll see flowers growing," she told the child.

Materials
   empty coffee cans
   paint
   paintbrush
   stickers or a magazine with pictures of birds or flowers
      (or cut out the flower on the seed package)
   glue
   spoon
   potting soil
   seeds

   Note: Marigolds, forget-me-nots, daisies, violets, and
      herbs are easy to grow.

Directions

   1. Peel the label off the can and wash the can thoroughly.
   2. If you place one hand inside the can you can paint with the other. Paint all around the can but leave the bottom unpainted. You might like to paint bands of different colors to make a rainbow.
   3. Wash the brush in water before using different paint colors.
   4. Put the can aside to dry for about ten minutes.

5. Decide where you want to put the decorations and paste sticker designs around the can. Or cut out a design from the magazine and glue it in place.
6. Use the spoon to fill the can about two inches from the top with the potting soil.
7. Drop a few seeds on top of the dirt. Spoon in another inch of dirt on top of the seeds. Don't fill the can all the way to the top.
8. Pour a little bit of water, not too much, into the planter to wet the seeds.
9. Place the can in a sunny spot. Wait for seeds to sprout.

Remind your grandchild to water the dirt again when it gets dried out. Tell her that soon she will have her very own tiny garden growing right in her room. Show her the picture of the flowers that will bloom. When the stems are about two inches tall, the plants can be repotted in flowerpots or transplated outdoors if the weather is warm enough (see directions on the seed package).

Toy Tote

Callie has lots of toys with little pieces that she leaves at her grandparents' house. One day her grandfather was painting the trim on his house when he got an idea. The cardboard paint bucket that held the paint would be perfect for holding the little toy pieces and would make a great project for Callie.

The next time he went to the hardware store, he bought several paint pails in different sizes. At home he let Callie paint the outside of these pails with the latex paint he was using for the house trim. Then he said, "What is your favorite fruit?" When she said it was an apple he said, "Why don't you paint a big red apple on one side of your paint pail."

He got out the small bottles of craft paint and let her design her own apple that included a stem, green leaves, and yellow polka dots. Then he suggested that she paint a yellow banana next to it. She decided to paint a pink banana instead, followed by green cherries, and a purple ice-cream cone. They put the finished project aside to dry and later Callie filled it with all her toy pieces. If she wants to decorate more pails, they can be used to neatly hold mittens, toys, or the pretend food from her play kitchen.

Pretty Hand Mirror

Four-year-old Patty was playing paddleball when the elastic snapped and the ball flew off. "What a good opportunity,"

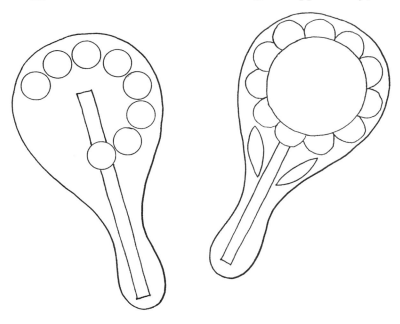

Grandma consoled the crying child. "We're going to use this paddle to make your very own flower mirror for looking at yourself close up."

Together they assembled a round lacy doily that would become the petals around the mirror, a small hand-mirror from Grandma's purse, a piece of green construction paper, and craft glue to make the stem and leaves.

If you don't mind the messiness of painting, your grandchild can first paint the front of the paddle. If not, simply make this a cut-and-paste project. For painting, if you put the paddle on wax paper the child can paint the paddle and leave it to dry without sticking.

On the green construction paper, draw two lines about a half inch apart and as long as the paddle. This is the stem. Let your grandchild cut this out. Draw two petal shapes for leaves and let the child cut these out.

Next, spread glue on the back of the stem strip. Place it down the center of the paddle and press down. Wipe away excess glue with a damp sponge. Now spread glue on the back of the doily and press it onto the round, top part of the paddle, right over the top part of the stem. Spread glue on the back of the hand mirror and set in the center of the doily. Press down and let dry thoroughly so it won't slide down when you pick up the paddle. Glue the leaves on each side of the stem wherever the child thinks they look best.

As a substitute for the doily you can use those self-sticking dots that come in packages of different sizes and colors in stationery stores. Place the mirror in the center of the paddle top and draw around it with a pencil. Remove the mirror and place a sticker dot on the drawn line so it overlaps the line a little on the outside edge. Continue to add dots, overlapping them a little bit all the way around the line. These will form the petals around the mirror.

Patty personalized her mirror with her name. She used a

package of gummed gold letters from the five-and-dime and lined them up to spell her name on the back of the paddle.

Picture Me

Use a child's school picture to decorate a metal cough drop tin to hold such treasures as a bracelet or rings or tiny rocks and shells. First she paints the top of the tin, then centers and glues her picture on the top. Tell your grandchild this is her personal treasure box, and because her picture is on it, this identifies it as hers alone. If she wants, she can add sticker designs around her picture to make it fancy.

Aircraft

Orly, a former airline pilot, likes to teach his grandchildren the simple principles of aerodynamics through making things that fly. He recently told his small grandson, Willie, "Air is everywhere. You can't see it, but you can feel it when the wind blows. Birds use air for transportation. A paper airplane can glide on the air just like a bird."

The craft projects he makes with his grandchildren all use air to move. One of his easiest projects is a paper airplane designed for distance gliding, and it has won many awards. You and your grandchild can make it anytime you feel like flying a paper plane. He says, "You may find this is the best plane you or your grandchild has ever made."

Materials
   8½ × 11-inch paper
   markers or crayons
   tape

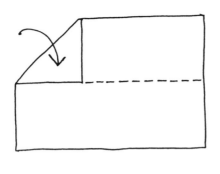

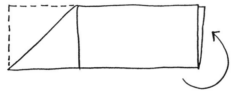

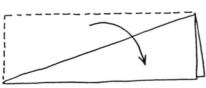

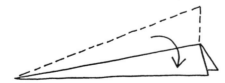

Directions

1. Draw a design on the paper. It can be a curvy line from the top to the bottom of your paper. Follow that line with another line in a different color. Leave a white space between the colored lines.
2. Continue doing this until the paper is covered with colored and white stripes going in a squiggly direction.
3. Turn the paper over and fold it in half lengthwise. Open the paper flat again, design side down.
4. Fold the top two corners in, a little short of the center crease.
5. Fold the paper on the center line in the opposite direction of the first fold.
6. Take the bottom corner and fold it back to the center fold. Turn the plane over and do this on the other side.
7. Repeat step 6, folding once more down the center fold.
8. Angle the wings up slightly. Tape the underside of the plane together to prevent it from opening. Use a small piece of tape on top to hold the wings together.

Hold the glider from underneath and give the plane a gentle push to steady its flight. It will glide straight and smoothly for a long distance. Your colorful design will look beautiful sailing through the air. The more you practice, the farther your plane will glide.

Model Planes

Pop Pop Jon reports that the little dime-store balsa wood airplanes are easy to put together and fun to play with outdoors. "Sometimes the kids paint them with decorative designs before putting them together," he says. "But," he warns, "be sure to buy more than one. They always seem to get stuck in a tree, totally beyond retrieval."

Make a Skimmy

One summer day, surrounded by grandchildren and in need of a project to keep them busy, Jon invented his own version of a Frisbee, which he calls a Skimmy. It's made of paper, and the kids can decorate it any way they like. When tossed into the air it spins on its way back to you. A Skimmy is made of Fome-Cor, a special kind of paper you buy in an art supply store. If you can't find it, use stiff white cardboard. One sheet of Fome-Cor is enough to make several skimmies.

Directions

1. Have your grandchild place a large bowl or round plate on top of the Fome-Cor and, using a marker, trace around it.
2. Next, you can carefully cut out the circle for him with a craft knife.
3. Let him decorate the Skimmy by using smaller, different-size cans and bowls to draw circles on each side. He can use markers or crayons to color in the circles to create a bright pattern.

Take the Skimmy to an open area. Toss it as hard as you can into the air directly above you. It will whirl and fly in different directions before landing. Keep it away from trees and rooftops, or it might get lost before he has a chance to give it a whirl. And never throw it at someone.

When he tosses the Skimmy into the air, the colored circles will blend together.

 ## Simple Games

Four-year-old Miles loves to play the card game war with his grandfather. However, he doesn't always stick to the rules. Sometimes he isn't sure which numbers are highest, and he takes the pile with confidence even when he hasn't won. His grandpa always lets him win. On the other hand, Allison at eight expects Grandpa to be a worthy chess adversary.

Hide-and-Seek

Len loves to play hide-and-seek with his three-year-old granddaughter, Marissa. He makes a big show of looking under tables, chairs, and behind the curtains. "Is Marissa under the table? No, not here," he announces, while dragging out this little charade. He tells me, "She's usually standing in plain sight with her hands over her eyes until I exclaim, 'Here she is!' It amuses me how many times we can do this without her losing interest." One day Marissa said, "Poppy, let's play hide-and-seek and all hide together!" Children this age clearly don't care about the rules of the game. Do it their way. When they are a little older they understand the concept of hiding and finding and participate just as enthusiastically. This simple activity gives you both a chance to get exercise and fresh air, and it keeps a child busy and happy for a while. Parents don't always have time for this simple fun.

Ring-Around-the-Rosy

Martin learned a valuable lesson while baby-sitting for his two-year-old grandchild. "Never teach two-year-olds how to play ring-around-the-rosy unless you have the energy to fall down yourself, over and over again. They are never the first to tire of this game."

Indoor Volleyball

It was a rainy weekend, and Florence's grandchildren were restless from being cooped up in her small apartment. "Let's play volleyball," she announced. They couldn't believe that Grandma would let them play this game in the living room. Then she told the children to push all the chairs against the walls and clear a space. She tied a string between the backs of two chairs and blew up a balloon. The youngest child and Florence formed one team against the two oldest children while Grandpa kept score. "Their interest in the game lasted just long enough to let off some steam before dinner," Florence says.

Beanbag Tag

Jim is a single grandfather. Whenever he saw his three- and five-year-old grandsons in the past, his wife had provided things for them to do at their house. Now he was taking care of them alone and realized he had nothing for them to play with. He created this simple game of beanbag tag.

You'll need two small self-seal plastic bags, uncooked beans or rice, an old pair of socks (this is a good way to get rid of those unmatched singles), and two rubber bands. Fill each bag with half a cup of uncooked beans or rice.

Squeeze the air out of the bags, leaving enough room for the beans to move around. Seal the bags. Stuff the bags into the old socks and secure with an elastic band around the ankles. Cut off the excess sock.

Arrange an obstacle course with chairs, tables, and other pieces of furniture that can't topple over. Choose one person to be it. Both players put the beanbags on top of their heads. The object is to tag the other person without losing the bag from one's head while navigating the obstacle course. The goal is to get to the designated safety zone without being tagged or losing your beanbag. Jim says, "The kids came up with all sorts of variations for this game. It kept them busy all afternoon. They gave me the handicap of having to play on my knees. They loved that."

Card Games

Bud has taught all six of his granddaughters all sorts of card games. This is a standard part of the activities they expect to do when they visit. When they were little, Bud and the girls made up games such as matching all cards of the same color, or grouping cards with the same numbers, and variations on all the traditional card games. "Of course they all made up their own rules and it usually changed with each hand. They never told me what the rules were, only that I lost. Somehow it was never my turn to win," he says.

Grandpa Bud and Grandma Mat (their shortened version for Madeline) have introduced lots of activities revolving around nature. "We always pick berries in the summer and make jam and pies," Mat says. "When we go to the beach at low tide we take big buckets and rakes and dig for clams," Bud adds. "Then we steam them at home and the girls really enjoy opening and eating them. But," he says, "after any activity, someone always sets up a card game. The cards are left on the table for a quick pick-up game of

go fish, crazy eights, war, or their version of poker, at a moment's notice."

Action Fun

Grandparents of little ones know that "I'm a Little Tea-pot" is a winner, if they can do a good job of turning into a teapot and pouring themselves exactly on cue. For those who have forgotten and want to be au courant with a two-year-old, here's how it goes:

Sing: *I'm a little teapot short and stout.* (Bend knees outward on the word *stout.*)

Here is my handle. (Put one hand on hip to form a rounded handle.)

Here is my spout. (Put other hand crooked out from your body to form the spout.)

When I get all steamed up hear me shout, tip me over and pour me out. (Lean to the handle side on *tip* and to the spout side as if you're pouring yourself on the word *pour*.)

Outdoor Fun

James thinks every grandparent should invest in a soccer ball. "Not just any rubber ball," he says, "but a real soccer ball. It will provide endless hours of fun for all ages. When I play with my three- and four-year-old grandchildren we don't have any rules. I just let the kids make up the game as they kick the ball around the yard." Once four-year-old Tony said, "Let's see who can hit the tree," and this became the point of the game. James says, "At other times we put a stick down and each child tries to kick the ball over this line. Sometimes they take turns seeing who can kick the farthest, or they just kick it every which way." He points out that games involving children of this age should never have winners and losers, just action. Everyone is a winner.

Old McDonald's Farm

Grandpa Horace knows how to make all the animal sounds exactly right and can insert them in the correct sequence in the song "Old McDonald's Farm." His little grandchildren delight in making the appropriate sounds for the animals. "Once we've gone through all the obvious animals they know, like pigs, horses, dogs, cats, ducks, it's fun to see how long you can go on making up new animals and sounds," he says. "After we've exhausted the list, we make up words for imaginary animals and invent sounds to go with them. The kids anticipate the silliness of this game and can't wait to get to this part."

Hokey-Pokey

All the interactive games that kids love can be improvised to make up a version of your very own. For example, Horace also has the kids get in a circle to sing "The Hokey-Pokey," and they love finding new body parts to shake up. If you've forgotten this one, here's how it goes. As each of the directions is sung, you put the appropriately named body part into the center of the ring.

You put your right hand in. (Everyone sticks out the right hand. "Do not correct a grandchild for sticking out his left hand," Grandpa suggests.)

You put your right hand out. (Put your right hand in back of you.)

You put your right hand in and you shake it all about. (With your arm in front of you, shake it as hard as you can. "The harder you shake, the more they love it," he says.)

You do the hokey-pokey and you turn yourself around. (Wiggle your body and shake yourself up, then twirl around.)

And that's what it's all about. (Everyone claps.)

Next it's your left hand. Horace says, "Continue to put in knees, elbows, behinds, heads, left and right feet, and anything else you can think of like noses, tongues, ears, chin, teeth, hair, and so on, until the grandchildren have had enough. Be as silly as you want, with such items as pinkies, thumbs, blinking eyelashes, and belly buttons."

Creative Drawing Game

This is fun for two or more children. You will need plain paper and colored pencils or crayons. The first child draws a line on the paper. Using another color, the next child adds a line or a shape. Children continue taking turns until they have completed a picture. Then they color in the drawing.

 ## Stories and Songs

While children love having books read to them, hearing made-up stories is even more fun. "My grammy tells me stories about when she was a little girl and didn't even have a television set!" Elizabeth says in amazement. Old songs, family stories, and bedtime lullabys help create a bond with grandparent and grandchild and provide special moments to share.

Storytelling

My granddaughters love to hear stories about when their parents were little, about when they were babies, and about when Nana and Pop Pop were little. But their favorite story is called "Mommy and Daddy Get Married." They love to hear every detail about Mommy walking down the aisle in her beautiful wedding dress with the veil and carrying a bouquet of flowers. They ask over and over about the flower girl, and they love the part when the minister asks the questions and Daddy kisses Mommy. It is a very dramatic tale that ends with everyone throwing rose petals and Mommy and Daddy going off on their honeymoon.

All Stories Have Happy Endings

Suzanne tells her grandchildren the traditional fairy tales, but she always changes inappropriate parts, and all stories have happy endings. For example, "I modify the oven scene in 'Hansel and Gretel' as well as the eating scene with the wolf in 'Little Red Riding Hood.' I would never have the wolf eat Grandma, even if the hunter does cut him open to rescue her."

BethAnn's grandchildren have a stepmother, and she studiously avoids telling the tale of Cinderella. "When it comes to Rumplestilskin, I refer to him as a little person, never a dwarf," she says.

Interactive Songs

"We all know that repeating nursery rhymes such as 'London Bridges,' 'Patty-Cake,' or 'Ring-Around-the-Rosy' delights little children," says Laura, a librarian and grandmother of four children under four. "To really get the most out of the song, keep the child physically involved. Just wiggling a little toe while you sing 'this little piggy' holds his attention." She says that rhymes help children listen, and listening skills build a foundation for reading skills. "If you just talk to them, they tune out, and besides, their level of understanding is quite limited. Rhymes enable you to communicate and interact."

Some grandparents sing old songs from their childhood

that children don't hear today. My mother sings songs like "K-K-K . . . Katie" and "Mairsy Dotes" and "Bicycle Built for Two" to her great-grandchildren, and they always beg for more.

 # Outings

All grandparents enjoy an outing with their grandchildren. Careful planning will ensure success and fun for all.

Camping Out

From the time his grandson was born, Louis dreamed of taking him camping as he had done with the child's father many years before. He imagined what it would be like showing the boy how to set up the tent, then catch a fish and cook it over a fire. They would roast marshmallows, and he'd tell the boy stories about camping with the boy's father when he was the same age. This sort of dream can turn out to be a perfect reality, or not.

When the boy was six his parents consented to an overnight trip. Louis and his grandson didn't catch any fish, but they did cook the eggs and bacon they'd brought along for breakfast. The ground was harder than Louis remembered from the last time he'd gone camping many years ago, and he didn't get much sleep. As for the male bonding over the fire, the boy was asleep by seven o'clock and the adventure turned out to be rather adventureless. "Next time I think we'll go to Disney World and wait to try camping again in a few years," he concluded.

The Ballet

When Becky was six her grandmother took her to a local ballet school recital. The child dressed up in her best party clothes and they had tickets in the front row. As the lights dimmed and the music began, Becky leaned over and said, "Isn't this exciting, Nana?" Her grandmother had always dreamed of taking her to *The Nutcracker* or *Swan Lake*, but this was the best she could offer and, at that moment, realized that it was every bit as wonderful in Becky's eyes.

Sunday Brunch

The grandparents of a four-year-old expressed the desire to take their grandchild out for brunch. This may seem like a great idea from the grandparents' point of view, but most four-year-olds prefer the petting zoo to Sunday brunch at a fancy restaurant. It's a good idea to check with your grandchild's parents before making reservations at a four-star restaurant.

Mall Savvy

Mall savvy is not something every grandparent is born with. This is a learned skill and one worth acquiring, according to suburban grandparents Amy and Steve. "In our town the mall is the center of activity. This is where the kids like to go for lunch at McDonald's, to see Santa at Christmastime, to the toy store, the candy store, and for some running around when they've been cooped up. We like to go there too because there's always something we need."

Before attempting this trip, however, they suggest knowing the safest place to park your car. This is usually near an entrance to the store. Find out the location of all the public bathrooms. "It doesn't matter if everyone goes to the potty before leaving home, someone always has to go the second we get out of the car," Amy says. "It's also a good idea to know exactly where you are going and how long you intend to stay in each place. Keep track of your time because children get tired easily. We never seem to be at the exit nearest the car at exactly the moment one of them lies down on the floor and says, 'Carry me, Nana. I'm too tired to walk.'" And Steve reminds us, "Never ever let your grandchildren out of your sight for one second."

 ## Cooking With Grandchildren

In child language, boiling water is cooking. Anything you do after that is beyond the call of duty. In other words, the simpler the better for all concerned.

Making Cookies the Way Your Grandma Didn't

This is the nineties. Nobody, not even a grandparent, has time to bake from scratch. Cutting off slices of Pillsbury cookie dough and popping it into the oven is the way a cool grandparent provides a great time. Kids don't know about the way it used to be, nor do they care. When they grow up they will remember making cookies with Grandma, not how it was done. The important thing is to have fun and remember that children have a short attention span.

Cleanup Is Cool

Cool grandparents don't care if things get messy. Cleaning up can be fun if you treat it as a special activity. Give one child a wet sponge to clean the counters. Let another child put away pots and pans on bottom shelves. Teach the children how to fold the dishtowels. A three-year-old child loves to empty the dishwasher and is capable of putting spoons and forks in the specified drawer.

Don't Fret If You're Not Into Cooking

Making hot chocolate is an activity any child enjoys. If done properly, it takes more involvement than you can imagine and provides an endless source of entertainment, over and over again, each time you do it. It's amazing how combining just two ingredients can involve so many steps.

Materials
   hot chocolate mix
   water
   small saucepan
   measuring cup
   teaspoon
   pretty teacup and saucer
   marshmallow fluff, miniature marshmallows, or whipped
      cream in a spray can

Directions

   1.   Pull a chair or stepstool up to the counter so your grandchild can get up to the right height.
   2.   Have the child measure a cup of water and pour it into the saucepan.

3. Turn the heat up to high. It will take only seconds to heat up. Do not bring to a boil, as most children don't have the patience to wait for the cocoa to cool enough to drink. If it gets too hot, have cold milk on hand.

4. While waiting for the water to heat, have the child measure a heaping teaspoon of cocoa into the teacup. Then you add the water while the child mixes with the teaspoon.

5. Serve with a dainty cookie on the side and a real napkin. This turns an ordinary activity into a special event.

6. Let the child add a heaping teaspoon or more of marshmallow fluff or a few marshmallows or whipped cream.

The Proper Tea Party

When Tara was three and Drew four, their grandmother introduced them to the art of the proper tea party. Since it was summertime, she set the table out on the patio. First she covered it with a floor-length pink linen tablecloth. Each child's place setting held a matching linen napkin tied with a ribbon under which she tucked a rosebud. In the center of the table Grandma filled a small vase with fresh roses from the garden.

Tea (which can also be lemonade or cocoa) was presented in a silver teapot along with a silver pitcher of milk and a sugar bowl. The best silverware was used, and each child had a pretty plate with a delicate teacup and saucer at his and her places. Another plate held several perfectly iced cupcakes from the bakery. Making cupcakes is an activity for another day, as is making lemonade.

Grandma piled the children's chairs with plump cushions so they'd be high enough to reach the table. Then she set a place for herself and they all sat down to enjoy a formal tea party. Grandma let Tara pour the tea into each teacup as she held it for her. Some spilled into the saucers, but it didn't matter.

Affecting an exaggeratedly formal voice for their conversation, Grandma said to Tara, "You're looking particularly lovely this afternoon, Ms. Brown." "Thank you, Mrs. Grandma," replied Tara. "And what do you think about the weather, Mr. Brown? Will it rain?" "I don't think so," said Drew in a pronounced way, getting into the spirit of things. Grandma kept this up until they all began to make up silly words for things, creating their own particular tea-time conversation.

Now when Grandma says, "Who wants to have a tea party?" the children run to set the table as elaborately as they can. With small children it's so easy to create an enjoyable activity out of very little.

First You Take an Egg

Making hard-boiled eggs can be great fun for a four-year-old. Do not reserve this activity for Easter when you dye them. The act of peeling an egg is an activity in and of itself. This can easily take an hour, which will benefit you and your grandchild. Then let him eat any part that is appealing (some children won't touch the white, others won't eat the yellow). A cool grandparent doesn't care if they eat any of it. Making egg salad or deviled eggs are other activities to do together. Let them scoop the mayonnaise and mix it together. When they tire of this you can perfect it for consumption.

Fun Food to Make

There are lots of fun foods to make with your grandchildren. Sylvia's little ones especially like to make Jell-O Squiggles. Believe it or not, many parents today don't have time to make instant Jell-O and puddings. They buy them ready-made in little cups. Your grandchildren will love making instant anything, and by the way, this is called "cooking."

Scraping vegetables and filling celery sticks with peanut butter or cream cheese is fun and provides a healthful snack. Kids don't have to "cook" sweets to have a treat, and some parents don't particularly want their children to have sweets too often, especially between meals. Check with the parents about what the children can or can't eat. Don't assume that it's okay.

Avoiding the Heimlich Maneuver

Rule #1. Cheerios are round and won't get stuck in a nine-month-old throat.

Rule #2. Cornflakes will.

Rule #3. If they have no teeth, they can't eat anything that doesn't slide down smoothly, can't be sucked, or is larger than a Cheerio.

The Art of Serving Food to Grandchildren

I'm not sure when they develop this, but kids have very definite attitudes about food. While they vary slightly from child to child, most of what you'll learn is pretty universal.

The Peanut Butter and Jelly Issue

First you must know exactly what types of peanut butter and jelly are acceptable. Next it is crucial to know the exactly right ratio of peanut butter to jelly for a perfectly acceptable sandwich. If this is done incorrectly, keep your cool at all times because you will probably have to do this many times to get it right.

Favorite Foods

Molly offers advice about shopping for food before your grandchildren's arrival. "If you haven't a clue and think they're going to eat 'real food,' forget it. It may seem like an esoteric menu, but you'll be wise to stock the following items: french fries, American cheese slices (yellow and white—they always have an absolute preference and it will definitely be the one you didn't get, if you get only one, so get both), strawberries or grapes (even out of season), yogurt (plain and flavored), skim or 2 percent milk, chicken nuggets, frozen pizza, plain white bread, peanut butter and jelly, baby peas, and a large box of Cheerios. You'll be set for any meal."

Hold the Crust

It could be very useful to brush up on the following skills:

1. Learn how to cut a piece of toast into bite-size squares of the exactly right dimensions. Don't worry about what is "right." Your grandchild will let you know by stuffing three into his mouth at once. You will then realize that you must cut three tiny pieces to equal the size of one.
2. Learn how to construct a sandwich: Remove the crust and make an exact diagonal cut.
3. Know there is only one right way to do this and you will probably have to do it several times before getting it right. Know, too, that you will be judged by the highest critic.
4. Accept the fact that after you get it just right, he will take two bites and be done.

Keeping an Open Mind

When Theresa and Walter asked if they could take their grandson, Gregory, out to dinner, his mother warned them that, "A six-year-old doesn't consider dinner in a restaurant a lot of fun." But they were persistent, knowing they could have fun doing anything with him.

Mom suggested McDonald's or the local pizza place. This didn't appeal to Theresa and Walter, who wanted to take the boy to a nice restaurant. They chose a place where the chef makes a big show of cooking the food in front of the customers on an open fire. Gregory was mesmerized, they served child-size portions, and everyone had a great meal and a good time.

The Sophisticated Palate

Sara and Julia are used to eating in restaurants, and their parents have sophisticated palates. The girls are encouraged to sample a variety of foods, and I am always surprised when I find them eating something that I consider pretty esoteric for little children. They adore spicy foods. Their father likes to cook and doesn't mind letting them taste and reject foods they don't like. When their father's parents came to baby-sit, Grandma asked the girls what they'd like for dinner. She suggested spaghetti or hamburger. Giving it some thought, the girls finally announced, "We'd like moo shu pork tonight." As many of us have learned the hard way, modern kids often have quite sophisticated tastes, and you may be surprised by what they like. The girls' grandma says, "To be on the safe side, ask their parents what they like to eat. Don't assume they'll taste something new and exotic, or that they won't!"

Finicky Eaters

On the other hand, Gladys would be happy if her grandchildren ate *anything*. "No matter what they are served they push it away. Sometimes their mother makes two or three different meals for them before they'll take a bite of anything. I can't stand to watch this," she says. When they come to her house she tries all different kinds of things to entice them. Here are a few ideas she suggests for finicky eaters:

1. Create clown faces on the plate with pieces of vegetables, grated cheese, and thin slices of meat.
2. Stuff celery sticks with cream cheese, peanut butter, or tuna or egg salad.

3. Serve food with dips. For example, let them dip veggie sticks into yogurt or creamy salad dressing.
4. Cut sandwiches with cookie cutters for a variety of small shapes.
5. Arrange different-colored foods on a plate. My daughter cuts cucumber rounds, carrot slices, apple wedges, or strips of green pepper to put alongside the chicken or hamburger dinner. And she recommends small amounts. They can always ask for more.
6. Cut the food into bite-sized pieces and insert little flags on toothpicks for the kids to pick up and eat with. Note: Toothpicks aren't safe for kids under five.
7. Serve the string beans first and tell him the hot dog will be ready soon. In this way he's faced with the vegetable when he's most hungry.
8. Let him squirt ketchup or mustard from a squeeze bottle onto the hot dog by himself (with guidance so he doesn't drown it).
9. Put food coloring next to the salt and pepper. Sometimes orange cream cheese or purple mayo just tastes better. Make sure they use just a drop or two and don't dump the whole bottle in!
10. Don't make a big fuss if they don't eat much after you've gone to the trouble to prepare it.

Gladys reports that the last time she made dinner for her grandchild, she cut and arranged each food group in an interesting way on the plate. Satisfied, she put the enticing presentation before him. The child took one look and pushed the plate away. "What's the matter?" she asked. "They're touching," he said. No matter what she did, as far as he was concerned the food had *already* been contaminated. "Children hate it when foods touch. Try serving foods in different containers or on different plates," she suggests. If you have TV-dinner-type plates with separated sections for each type of food, use these.

An exception to the no-touching rule are foods that must touch. Some children won't eat peas and mashed potatoes unless they are mooshed together. Unfortunately, adults are incapable of knowing which foods are which.

Don't Make Dessert a Reward

Mothers today are more enlightened than we were. Tempting as it might be, it is no longer appropriate to say, "Eat your spinach or you won't get dessert." The experts tell us that this may work in the short run, but in the overall scheme of developing good eating habits, this sends out a message about what is "good" food and what is "bad." We don't usually keep junk food in our house and try to offer fruit or yogurt along with meals. Here are some fun ways with food that have worked with our grandchildren:

1. Let the kids help make their dinner, choosing foods that are all the same color. Or have them pick food in their favorite colors to see how many different things they come up with.

2. Take them to the supermarket with you to pick what they want to eat. Then go right home to make the meal. If you wait until tomorrow, they won't want it anymore. Also, don't buy anything that, once cooked, doesn't bear any resemblance to the way it looked in the store.

3. Serve milk in a small pitcher beside their glasses so they can pour a little in at a time. Small children love to pour. Be sure they are eating where spills can be cleaned up easily.

4. Make a shish kebab meal of small pieces of meat or chicken and vegetables on a skewer.

5. Let the kids make a sundae with vanilla or plain yogurt, raisins, cherries, and granola or pieces of cold cereal. Let them sprinkle cinnamon over the top.

6. Adding whipped cream, especially from an aerosol can, to anything is fun for kids. Cut slices of fruit such as rounds of banana and slices of peaches or pears and let them squirt a little bit of whipped cream on top.

7. Seat the child's favorite dolls or animals around the table as well and give everyone a plate with a small portion of the child's dinner on it. Tell your grandchild you hope everyone clears his or her plate. Then turn to do other things in the kitchen while saying, "I wonder if Teddy likes his peas." The child will usually eat the peas in order not to disappoint you. Then turn around and say, "My goodness, he ate every one of them. But I see Barbie didn't eat her carrot stick." Before you know it, your grandchild will have eaten part, if not all, of a complete meal— maybe.

We All Have Our Limits

Since he was having trouble getting his grandson to eat, Mike checked the Internet for information that might be helpful. This is what he says, "I learned that keeping a finicky eater at the table longer will not make him eat more. In fact it works in the opposite way." He says it helps to ask your grandchild's parents the following questions the next time you're in charge of feeding him:

1. What should I do if he leaves the table?
2. Should I keep the plate of food on the table for later? Will he return when he's hungry?
3. Should I reheat the food after it's gotten cold?
4. What if he doesn't eat dinner and then says he's hungry before going to bed? What should I offer?
5. What if he doesn't eat at all?

He suggests, "Don't wait until the incident occurs, and don't make up your own rules. Ask your grandchild's parents how they want you to handle this and do it their way. It's easier when everyone is consistent."

Hot Breakfast Ritual

Edward always gets up early and delights in making breakfast for his two grandchildren when they come to visit. Their parents love it too, as this gives them a chance to sleep late. "I make a big to-do about cooking oatmeal, all the while exclaiming about how I can't wait to enjoy this delicious breakfast. I put out maple syrup and the sugar bowl and some cinnamon and carefully cut up bananas, then fill a bowl with blueberries or whatever is in season. I then have the children get out the place mats and our favorite bowls and set the table. By the time we sit down to breakfast they are all primed. One morning, however, the youngest said he didn't like oatmeal anymore. I simply told him that's all we had and that was that. I know their mother often makes different things for them, but I don't do that," he said.

However, that afternoon Edward took the boys shopping and let each pick out his favorite cold cereal to keep in the house. "Next time, when one of you doesn't want Grandpa's oatmeal, you can have your own cereal," he told them. It was an easy solution.

Baby's First Finger Food

Rose and Lewis like to baby-sit for nine-month-old Zachary. "If you want to be welcome in your daughter-in-law's home," she advises, "never criticize her parenting skills, even in the most subtle way."

When Grandma and Grandpa offered to baby-sit, Zachary's mother gave them explicit instructions not to give him any finger food. "It's too messy and he may choke." As a professional in child care education, Rose knows that at this age the baby needs to develop eye-hand motor coordination. Reaching for a biscuit, picking up Cheerios, and putting mashed banana in his mouth are important parts of his development. But she knew she shouldn't say anything or they would never leave her alone with the baby.

This is how she solved the problem. When she and Lewis went to visit, she brought along the foods in question. That evening she asked, "How would you feel if I gave him a biscuit?" And, "Would you mind if I watched him carefully while he eats a few Cheerios and banana for breakfast?" Always ask permission, she suggests. Never just give the child what you think he should have. Then she offered to get up early with Zachary so his parents could sleep late. In this way she was able to introduce the new foods without his mother hovering over him. "He loved it," she reports. "Eye-hand coordination is more important than getting nutrition from solid foods at this age. A nine-month-old baby gets all the nutrition he needs from his formula or breast milk. So that's not the issue. Now his mother trusts me and lets us feed him at our house where, I must admit, he has a wonderful time making a mess with his food."

9

Holiday Crafts

▼

We all love to make things related to the holidays, and it's most fun when we involve our grandchildren. Remember, whatever project you're working on, keep it extremely simple. If you have a project that you're doing for yourself, break it down into steps, designing one or two that can be done easily by a child. Don't start a project with them that they can't finish.

► **Christmas Decorations** ◄

If you don't make anything at any other time of year, Christmas brings out creative urges in most of us. Some grandparents make cookies and cakes with their grandchildren, others make decorations and gifts. The following ideas have all been grandchild tested and given the unofficial "Grandparent Seal of Approval."

Christmas Balls

I love to make fabric-covered balls to use as tree ornaments, and it's a project most children can handle.

Materials

    bag of Styrofoam balls (available in craft stores)
    scraps of green and red fabric (can be solids and prints)
    several yards of ¼-inch red and green ribbon for hanging
       loops
    straight pins
    scissors

Directions

1. If children are old enough to use scissors, have them cut all the fabric into narrow strips (about ¼ inch wide). If they are too young for this, prepare all the fabric ahead of time.
2. Demonstrate how to place one end of a strip of fabric on the Styrofoam ball and secure it by inserting a pin straight into the fabric and pressing it into the ball.
3. The child holds the ball with one hand and, with the other, wraps the strip of fabric around and around the ball. When she comes to the end of the strip, she secures it with another pin. You may have to help by holding the ball while she sticks the pin in. Children love to stick pins in things.
4. Take another strip of the same fabric and secure it on the Styrofoam ball with another pin. Continue to wrap the Styrofoam in the same way until the entire ball is covered with fabric.

5. Cut 6- to 8-inch strips of ribbon. Fold each in half lengthwise to make a loop and cross the raw ends over one another. Hold the crossed ends of the ribbon in place on the ball while your grandchild pushes a pin through the ribbon ends into the ball to secure it. This is your hanging loop.

6. If you don't make loops for hanging, these decorative balls can be piled into a pretty container, such as a glass bowl or open-weave basket, and used as a decorative accessory on a table.

Note: A tomato pincushion is a favorite in our house. Always supervise its use. The kids love to arrange pins in the pincushion and I use quilt pins with colorful, round, plastic beaded heads for safety and easy handling.

Santa Cookies

Miranda makes Santa cookies with her grandchildren from one batch of vanilla dough. "The kids like to roll out the dough and cut out the cookies, then decorate them. So I make the dough and chill it before they arrive," she says. Every year she has a small Christmas tree in the kitchen, and the children decorate it with their cookies. "Somehow, by the time Christmas is over, the tree is looking mighty bare," she says. "It's funny, but I never see the cookies disappear."

Materials
  your favorite dough recipe or prepackaged dough
  1 tube red icing
  1 tube white icing
  Christmas-mix sprinkle sugar
  blue and pink sugar candy dots

wax paper
rolling pin
round cookie cutters
knife

Directions

Cookies
1. Preheat oven to 375 degrees.
2. Divide dough into batches, so each child has his or her own.
3. Roll out chilled dough between two sheets of wax paper to about ¼ inch thick.
4. Using a cookie cutter or mouth of a small jar, can, or drinking glass, cut out 3-inch round shapes.
5. Help the children to cut small triangles of dough to attach to the tops of each circle. This is the pointy top of Santa's hat. Curve the pointy end slightly.
6. Place the cookies 1 inch apart on a lightly greased baking sheet. Chill cookies in the freezer for ten minutes so they're firm. Before putting them in the oven, use the end of a skewer or chopstick to make a hole in the top of the hat for hanging.
7. Bake for 10 to 12 minutes, until lightly browned. Remove to wire racks and let cool.

Icing
1. If possible, give each child his or her own tubes of icing, to avoid squabbles.
2. Let each child cover the hat (triangle part of the cookies) with red icing. Outline the hat with white icing and add a pompon to the tip.
3. At the edge of the hat, with the white icing, squirt a rim of fluffy fur.

4. Cover the fur with sprinkles.
5. Use the white icing to make Santa's beard, mustache, and eyebrows. (Small children will need you to help by showing them where to place the icing to make the face.)
6. Put a blue candy dot on for eyes and a pink one for the nose. Put a dot of red icing on each side of the cookie to make Santa's cheeks.
7. Stick a toothpick through the icing to open the hole in the top of the cookie and thread each one for hanging on the tree.

► Gifts for All Occasions ◄

Birthdays, Mother's and Father's Day, and Christmas are all times that children like to have something to give their parents. When they come to your house, use these times as an excuse to do a simple crafting project with them. They will enjoy giving something they made, and many of these projects provide learning experiences.

Pomander Balls

This is an easy project for small children. Pomander balls can be made with a variety of fresh, firm fruit such as oranges, lemons, and limes. You'll also need a box of whole cloves. Pomander balls can be heaped in a bowl to sweeten the smell of a room or hung by a ribbon to freshen a closet.

Directions

1. Prepare the fruit by making holes with a skewer or toothpick around the skin. This makes it easier for the children to insert the clove stems.

2. Place a fruit on a piece of newspaper in front of each child.
3. Pour a handful of cloves onto the paper or into little cups for each one.
4. Demonstrate how to insert the cloves where you've pricked the skin.
5. Each piece of fruit should be covered with rows of cloves slightly spaced apart so the skin is showing between spaces.

For a spicy smell, put the pomander ball in a bowl and sprinkle with cinnamon. Or fill a bowl with the pomander balls and insert a few sprigs of greens for a pretty decoration.

This is a nice gift for children to give to their teachers. Have them gather a piece of tissue around the fruit and tie with a pretty ribbon.

Burr Basket

If you've ever taken a walk in the fields or woods you may have noticed that burrs stick to you. Your grandchildren might be fascinated to learn that burrs are seed pods and there are different kinds in different parts of the country. They all stick to you and to each other for a free piggyback ride, but they are harmless.

It's easy to make a burr basket. Gather a bag full of burrs, or you can make this project right in the field. Stick two burrs together. Keep sticking them together to form the shape of a small basket. When you have what looks like a little cup-size basket, add a handle made from more burrs stuck together.

This basket is not sturdy enough to carry by the handle, but you can fill it with dried flowers, red cranberries, or sprigs of holly for a table display. The children will have fun making it the next time you go walking in a field.

 ## Autumn Time

Many craft projects can teach your grandchildren about nature. Some of the projects we do in our family don't relate specifically to the holidays, but the materials we gather are available in nature at those particular times of the year. The fall, for example is a wonderful time to gather leaves and dried materials for wreath making or for decorating your Thanksgiving table. (See Family Gatherings on page 119 for more Thanksgiving projects.)

Gourd Bird Feeder

Gourds are funny-shaped objects that grow on vines and are part of the squash family, although they're not edible. They are beautiful in color and design and are always available in the fall at fruit stands and in supermarkets.

Your grandchildren might find it interesting to know that originally gourds were used as bowls, ladles, and cooking utensils. In colonial days they were used as water dippers, as cooking pots (by putting heated stones in them), and as fishing-net floats. Once dry, the seeds rattle around inside, and the gourd becomes a grand musical instrument. Indian snake charmers even used gourds as pipes.

Medium- to large-size gourds can be made into bird feeders that are perfect for chickadees. The gourds you use for crafting should be dry and hard. Draw a circle on the front of the gourd. An adult should then cut this out with a sharp knife. The inside has a soft ivory-colored, velvet-textured surface. The child can remove this by soaking the gourd in warm soapy water, then scraping it out with a spoon. The interior will feel like leather.

Punch a hole in the top with an awl, an ice pick, or a nail and let the child insert a wire or cord. Tie a knot to the inside and hang the other end of the cord to a tree. The child can then fill the gourd with birdseed. Before long the birds will be feeding happily from it.

Pine Sachets

If you live near a wooded area, you can collect pinecones and pine needles. If you break the pine needles into pieces they release a wonderful fresh smell. Pine needles usually blanket a woodland floor all summer. In the fall you can pick the dried needles from the trees in backyard areas as well, or, later in the year, use the needles from your soon-to-be-discarded Christmas tree. Use them to fill little cloth sacks for sweet-smelling pillows or sachets. Begin by gathering the dried pine needles, then let the children break them into small pieces. You'll need fabric that isn't so thin that the needles poke through (most cotton fabric is fine). This can be a simple sewing project or a no-sew project.

Directions

Sewing
1. Cut 2 pieces of pretty fabric approximately 4 inches square for a sachet, or 8 inches square for a pillow.
2. With right sides facing, stitch around three sides. You can do this on a sewing machine or by hand. I've found that a five- or six-year-old can do this

with a little help. My ten-year-old grandson loves to do simple projects like this on the sewing machine.

3. Turn the fabric right side out. Fill halfway with the pine needles. Tuck the raw edges of the fabric inside and stitch across to close the opening.

No-Sew
1. Cut a piece of fabric approximately 5 or 6 inches square.
2. Place it down with the wrong side up.
3. Put a small amount of the pine needles in the center of the fabric.
4. Gather the edges of the fabric around the needles and tie them together in a little bundle with a pretty ribbon. Insert a sprig of pine or dried herb into the bow if desired.

Spore Prints

Fresh, wild mushrooms can be used to make printed greeting cards. "There's nothing to it," says Grandma Ethel as she picks the fresh mushrooms that have sprouted in her garden after a rainy period. "The mushrooms do all the work." *Note*: Many mushroom species are poisonous, although all species can be handled. Wash hands carefully after touching them.

Materials
    construction paper or plain white paper
    mushrooms
    bowl
    fixative or hair spray

Directions

1. Gently remove the stem from the mushrooms so only the tops remain.
2. Place the mushrooms on the paper with the spore side down.
3. Cover with an inverted bowl. The mushroom releases spores onto the paper, making an interesting brown design. The bowl keeps air from disturbing the spores directly under the mushroom, which can cause a swirling effect.
4. Leave overnight. In the morning you'll have mushroom prints.
5. To preserve, spray with Krylon clear fixative or hair spray. Fold the paper to make a card.

Different shapes, sizes, and variety of designs can be achieved by arranging the mushrooms in different ways on the paper, such as close together, in a line, or in a circle.

Leaf Place Mats

While out for a walk in the park or playing in the yard, the children can collect a variety of fallen leaves.

Materials
   leaves
   construction paper
   glue
   clear Contact paper
   scissors

Directions

1. Arrange the leaves on the paper and glue each one in place. Younger children will do this in a rather haphazard way. Older children will take time to create a pleasing arrangement. Either way, don't make suggestions—it doesn't matter. The important thing is for them to do it their way.
2. Cut a length of clear Contact paper slightly larger than the construction paper. Place it on top of the leaves and let the child press it down and smooth it out. *Tip:* You can use a rolling pin or water glass to roll over the plastic paper and to remove any bubbles.
3. Turn the leaf place mat over and put another piece of Contact paper on the back. Smooth it down.
4. Trim the excess Contact paper all around.
5. Make several place mats to use for a Thanksgiving table.

 Egg-Citing Easter Eggs

Dying Easter eggs bright colors is easy enough to do with small grandchildren. However, it's not too much more work to decorate them with unique designs.

Tie-Dye Eggs the Easy Way

While the eggs are boiling, prepare the cups of dye in warm water with a teaspoonful of vinegar in each. Cool the eggs by running cold water over them. Next, wrap rubber bands or white cording around the eggs every which way. Now when you place them into the dye baths, the areas covered by the rubber bands or cord will remain white, thus creating an interesting pattern on the eggs.

Personalized Easter Eggs

Use a grease pencil or a regular crayon to write each child's name, or draw a design on a plain hard-boiled egg. Then dye the eggs. The dye will not take where you've written with the pencil, and the child's name will show up in white.

 # Valentines

Use all sorts of sewing notions like buttons, scraps of ribbon, lace, fabric, and paper doilies to make valentines on construction paper. If your grandchildren are making valentines for their parents, they can even incorporate their own picture into a collage.

Personally Yours

Help the child to center and glue a doily onto a piece of colored paper. Then he can glue his own picture in the center of the doily. Next, cut pieces of ribbon to fit around the edges of the picture to create a frame and have him glue them in place. Add sequins, buttons, and other decorations all around the outside of the picture. Write a message inside.

Make a Perfect Heart

Show your grandchild how to make a perfect heart. Fold a piece of paper in half and draw half a heart coming off the fold. Cut on this line and unfold the paper. Your grandchild can color and decorate this, then glue it to a colored-paper background.

10

My Grandparents Are Really Cool Because . . .

I asked a group of children from varying backgrounds from different parts of the country what they liked or remembered most about their grandparents. There was no hesitation, and it came as no surprise that this generation of kids feels the same way about its grandparents as our generation felt about our own. Quite simply, grandparents are loved and considered cool for being who they are. We give them unconditional love. We have time for them and let them know they're appreciated. In short, just being there for our grandchildren is all we have to do to be loved, appreciated, and considered the coolest grandparents a kid could hope to have. It's so much easier than being a parent! Here's what the kids had to say.

Annie says, "What I remember about my grandfather is the way he gave out dollar bills all the time—a dollar for a neat room, a dollar for a good report card. I was rich by the end of his visits. My grandma was a fabulous cook. Every time she visited, she cooked up a storm and left many meals behind when she went home. After she died, we had one of her casseroles in the freezer and we could hardly bring ourselves to eat it as it was her last gift to us."

Molly says, "My grandfather is a very loving and happy person. He plays the banjo in a band and is always singing and laughing. He and my grandmother are wonderfully supportive of everything my sister and I do and are always eager to hear from us. They are the best grandparents any kid could have!"

Jennifer says, "My grandma makes me feel really special. Every year she makes me the most elaborate birthday cake, decorated with fresh flowers from her garden."

Katherine says, "My grandmother lives far from us. Every fall she sends us leaves from her yard and I save them. From time to time I take out the leaves one by one and try to picture her yard and her house, which is where my dad grew up. I imagine him raking leaves like these in Grandma's yard with his dad when he was a little boy."

"My grandpa and I watch a dance program together on TV. We try to do the dances together. Grandpa picks me up and whirls me around the living room," says five-year-old Sheri. "I put my feet on the tops of his shoes and we dance around until the music stops. I think I'll marry Grandpa."

Lonnie says, "My grandparents are really old and I learn a lot from them. Grandpa and I sit out on the front porch talking about things. We listen to the birds and he can imitate them."

Eight-year-old Madeline says, "My grandma lives in Scotland, but she comes to stay with us for a month every summer. I call her Mima because when I was little I couldn't say Grandma. She travels to lots of places and brings me things from all over the world. But most of all I like to hear her stories. She says when I'm older I can come to stay with her for the summer."

"Every year we drive from Michigan to Florida to see my grandma. We stay for two weeks, and when it's time to leave Grandma and I get very sad," says twelve-year-old Randy. "She sends us home with a box filled with homemade cookies that I usually eat in the car. I think about her all the way home. When we get home we call her and I tell her how much I miss her and love her. I'll be so happy to see Grandma in heaven, and I know she'll be making cookies in the kitchen there when I arrive."

Sally says, "My grandpa is the greatest! He's always there when I need him and he always has time for me. I will always love him."

Theda, age six, says, "My granddaddy lives far away from the city where we live. In the country, where he lives, everyone knows everyone, and when I go for a ride in the car with him, they all wave to us as we pass by. I wave back. We go to the diner for breakfast, just the two of us, and everyone says hello to Granddaddy, and he says, 'This is my little princess,' and everyone is very nice."

Wendy says, "My grandma is a doctor and she's teaching me to be independent. She always smells good. I want to grow up to be just like her."

Jeremy says, "My grandfather likes to take me and my brother swimming. We also go fishing in his dinghy. When we stay home he plays old songs on the piano and we sing along. He has a piano bench with hundreds of music sheets in it. If we tell him about a song we like, he buys the music sheet so we can sing it together. He's a wonderful grandfather."

Tony, age nine, says, "My grandfather drives me everywhere. When I go to his house he says, 'Where would you like to go today?' and no matter where I say, he takes me. Sometimes we go to a movie together, but most of the time he drives me to my friend's house or to the mall or to baseball practice. He's a builder and he's always busy, but he drops whatever he's doing to take me wherever I want to go. He's the greatest guy on earth."

Andrew, age ten, says, "Whenever Grandma MaryJane goes shopping, she asks me what I like to eat and she always has great stuff in her refrigerator. I go there every day after school, and when I come in she gets up from her computer and brings me doughnuts or cookies and root beer and we talk about my day. She has two dogs, and sometimes she hires me to take them for a walk or feed them. I stay there for an hour and then my mother or father comes to get me."

Jonny, at four years old, says, "My grandpa has a big, overstuffed chair. He lets me stand on my head in his chair. Nobody else sits in Grandpa's chair. It's our special place. Grandpa reads there and I stand on my head for a long time."

Seven-year-old Peter says, "My grandma and grandpa really love each other. They are always hugging and kissing. Grandma also loves candy. They have a candy dish that's always filled with different candies every time I go to their house. We go there every Sunday and I can't wait."

Dear Grandparents,

I'd love to hear from you if you'd like to share your memories and experiences. Drop me a note by mail, fax, or E-mail about the following:

1. What do you remember most fondly about your grandparents?
2. What do you love most about being a grandparent?

Thanks for sharing.

Fondly,

Leslie Linsley

Leslie Linsley
37½ Union Street
Nantucket, MA 02554

Fax: 508-325-5836
E-mail: Linsley@nantucket.net

Index

special events (*continued*)
See also family celebrations; holidays; vacations
special events (the new baby), 115–19
best gift, 117
big brother, big sister celebration, 117
christening or briss, 116–17
it's a boy!, 115
lie if you have to, 118–19
names are a personal matter, 115–16
overstaying welcome, 118
when new baby arrives, 118
spoiling. See presents (the spoiling issue)
stories, giving happy endings to, 164
storytelling, 163–64
Sunday brunch and grandchildren, 166
supermarket caper, 52–53
synthetic fabrics, 70–71

tea parties, 169–70
teenagers and clothes as presents, 67
television issue, 37–38
scary movies, 38
videos appropriate, 23–24
temper tantrums, 108
Thanksgiving weekend, 120–21
table settings by kids, 123
tie-dye flowers, 144–46
toast skills, 173
toddler's pleasure, 139
toy store code, cracking, 63
toy tote, 150–51
toys
buttons, 56
safe playthings, 55
special toys at your home, 35
yard sale toys, 135

See also presents
trust, developing, 78

vacations, 124–31
all together at the seashore, 125–26
away from home, 126
do your research, 127–28
a family affair, 125
fun for all, 127
going to a hotel, 128
resources, 130–31
room service, 128–29
sharing interests, 129–30
a week without parents, 130
valentines, 191–92
make a perfect heart, 192
personally yours, 191
videos
appropriate, 23–24
scary movies, 38
Visatours, 131
visiting (baby-sitting), 34–41
bedtime, all together, 40
bedtime, negotiating, 39–40
bedtime story, reading, 40
best days to baby-sit, 35–36
documenting your visit, 38–39
keeping them busy, 41
nap as survival technique, 39
scary movies, 38
sibling rivalry, settling, 40–41
special toys at your home, 35
sticking to the schedule, 36–37
television issue, 37–38
time stands still, 37
visiting (dressing), 42–44
color-coordinated, 42
naked is better, 43–44
refusal to dress, 43
snowsuit maneuver, 42–43
visiting (enjoying everyday things), 30–34
ongoing projects, 31–32
outdoor fun, 34